THE WORLD'S BEST
PHOTOGRAPHS

ICICLES   by **HANS STEINER**

The World's Best Photographs

ODHAMS PRESS LIMITED, LONG ACRE, LONDON, W.C.2

S. 1039

Printed in England by The Sun Engraving Co. Ltd., London and Watford, Herts.

CONTENTS

AUTUMN MORNING   by **HAROLD BURDEKIN**

INTRODUCTION

THE task of compiling a book which claims in its title to present its readers with the best of anything is a task that cannot be undertaken lightly. It does not matter whether the material the book contains is short stories, pictures or photographs; whatever the subject matter, to make such a claim in the title is simply to invite criticism.

In the second place, if such a claim is made at all the editor must perpetually face up to his own preferences. Is his selection of material to be governed by his own likes—that is, to be made from what he honestly considers to be the best— or is the selection of material to be governed by what he believes his readers will like?

If he adopts the former course he will inevitably offend the tastes and susceptibilities of many of his readers. He is fortunate if he does not offend the majority of his readers. If he adopts the latter course he is again backing his personal judgment and has no guarantee that he is right. Moreover he may frequently be prostituting his own conception of what is good to what he thinks other people will like.

Now between what people like and what is good there may be—indeed there frequently is—considerable divergence. Those who doubt this statement have only to remember that musical comedies are far more popular than the plays of Shakespeare; it is, none the less, the considered opinion not only of experts but also of the great mass of humanity that Shakespeare's plays are artistically much more worth while, much better, that is, than at least the great majority of musical comedies.

If, however, the task of compiling *The World's Best Photographs* was one that few might envy, it was a task that gave its editor and those who helped him a great deal of pleasure. It was undertaken in no cavalier spirit and indeed its preparation was begun as much as two years before the book finally appeared. During that two years some 8,000 photographs representing the work of nearly 700 photographers were collected in the editor's office. There are included in this present volume just over 400 photographs, and a simple calculation will show that of every 20 photographs received by me, I was compelled to reject 19.

I do not claim for a moment that those I have chosen are in every case better than those which I have rejected but my space was limited and

I do claim that those which I have chosen are magnificent photographs. Others would undoubtedly have made a different selection from mine and indeed several volumes could have been compiled without including the same photograph in any two of them.

I would like to express my thanks to all those photographers from all over the world, who have so kindly submitted their work to me (and very many of whom I have disappointed), but they have all shown a sympathetic understanding of the task I had in hand and my grateful thanks are theirs for this understanding even more than for the excellent photographs they were good enough to send me.

A subsidiary difficulty in preparing this book has been the problem of division. I felt that from every point of view it was better to divide this book into sections, though precisely how it was to be divided was extremely difficult. My final choice was quite arbitrary. With every justification I could have included very nearly all the 400 odd pictures appearing in this volume in the section that I have called "The Camera as Artist" for each of them is in my view a distinctive artistic achievement.

I was governed in my task of dividing up the book by considerations of easy reference and although I should be the first to admit that many pictures in different sections could well appear in several other sections without straining in the least the titles which those sections have been given, I do claim that the division adopted does make it easier for the reader to find his way about.

No index has been included in this book. I decided to omit it only after careful thought. Practically all of the titles chosen for the photographs which here appear were selected by me and not by the actual photographers. The titles are, therefore, quite arbitrary and anyone who wishes to refer to a particular picture would find an index useful only if he remembered first of all the name of the photographer who took it and secondly the title which I had ascribed to it. The chances of him remembering both these facts are very small in view of the large number of pictures here collected and an index, in consequence, seemed to me a useless encumbrance. I preferred, therefore, to devote the three or four pages which it would have occupied to more pictures.

THE EDITOR.

THE CAMERA LOOKS AT US

In this first section have been collected photographs primarily of human interest. They show us ourselves in all our moods, at work and at play. Here will be found delicate character studies of people of all ages from tiny children to greybeards; intimate "candid camera" shots and "conversation pieces" recording our unguarded moments, graphic action pictures captured anywhere, at the seaside, in stage and studio, in field or factory.

IT may be said to-day, with but little exaggeration, that each one of us is a photographer. There are the few who, with full studio equipment, make of photography their livelihood; there are the considerable number who from time to time earn an honest guinea by entering the photographic competitions which nearly every modern newspaper organises periodically; there are, finally, the countless thousands who with such simple cameras as the "Baby Brownie" get enormous enjoyment from taking "snaps" of "Mother and Dad" on holiday at the seaside and sometimes inflict considerable boredom by showing their albums to their friends when the holidays are over.

No longer now is it as fashionable as in former days to make attempts at singing, playing the piano, or painting in water-colours; instead, those creative energies that formerly went to satisfy them are now turned very largely to photography. And in America and France, and more recently in the rest of Europe, papers have been launched which sell on their photographs alone. Indeed, the rise of such papers is one of the romances of modern journalism. The public clamour for them, and ask for more, with an appetite that is apparently insatiable. We see the public taking photography to its bosom, becoming "camera conscious" in a big way, and giving every indication of becoming more so.

In Britain the "photo-journal" has progressed by leaps and bounds until it is almost abreast of its American rivals. Other countries have profited by the experience of the earlier ventures, and to-day all over the world new photographic journals are springing up. The East has made its own ventures. In India, in particular, are photographic journals which in modernity and style hold their own with anything in the world.

Of all the many branches of photography, it is safe to say that the type of picture that gave to camera-work its first great impetus is the one that shows us what we ourselves look like, for it panders, to an extent undreamed of before the day of the camera, to two of the most powerful emotions that human beings feel—those of curiosity and vanity. Before the dawn of photography this desire to see what we look like called forth the intimate, domestic type of picture which reached its full flower in Dutch art in the sixteenth century, and in the more stylised family groups, the "Conversation Pieces" of Gainsborough and the other great artists of the eighteenth-century English school.

The coming of the camera, however, has to a large extent shifted the demand for the "human interest" picture from the artist (used in this sense to denote a man who draws or paints) to the photographer. It is often said that "the camera cannot lie," and though in point of fact the camera can, on occasions, be made to tell the grossest lies, the photographer is, generally speaking, tied down, on account of the scientific nature of his medium, to what is actually in front of his camera.

One photograph is to the ordinary man or woman worth a page of description and can be made to carry more conviction than all the arguments of a modern Socrates. It is unthinkable that there should be produced as evidence in a court of law a painting by, say, Augustus John, of the room where the murder was committed; yet it is a fact that a large part of a cameraman's business in the Harlem district of New York, for example, is concerned with taking such things as "the bedroom ceiling that fell down," and "the black eye received in the fight," so that the results can be produced as irrefutable evidence in court.

It is only in very recent years, however, that the art of the candid or unposed type of photograph has really developed. Before this, photographers were hampered by their materials, by the lack of speed in plates and lenses, from getting anything but obviously posed pictures, those wooden groups, faces set in glassy stares, that gaze bleakly at us from the pages of so many family albums. Compare a representative photograph from such an album with the "Portrait Unaware" on page 27. The subtle and telling humour in the composition of the latter is of very recent development in photography.

During the nineteenth century, people became camera-conscious in the worst possible way, and this type of camera-consciousness has persisted, so that even to-day the mere sight of a camera is sufficient to produce in the demeanour and expression of many people a change as devastating as it is unnatural. They are being photographed, therefore

THE HELMSMAN   by **EUSTON SEALY**

they must pose and be self-conscious till the ordeal is over, when they can again revert to their normal selves. The results—and they are to be seen on practically every passport in the world—give about as adequate a rendering of the subject as would a picture of a brick wall.

As a result of this camera-consciousness the art of studio portrait photography has become as much a matter of psychology as of camera technique; the most essential part of the photographer's equipment is an ability to woo his subjects into a state of unselfconsciousness. How skilful the modern photographer has become in this psychological task may be seen in the child studies, formal as they are, on pages 38 and 39.

It is this necessity for unselfconsciousness in photographic subjects that has given rise to the "candid camera" in recent years. Instead of bringing his subjects into the studio, the modern photographer now goes out and catches them unawares. He works with a camera (almost as small as a watch and as precise in its mechanism) which he can carry about with him wherever he goes so that it is always at hand to catch and preserve the fleeting moment that makes a picture. He uses high-speed film that will not only catch the quick smile on a face, but will stop the bird on the wing, a train rushing by, the dancer as she leaps into the air.

By capturing these and similar moments for us he is performing one of the most useful functions of a true artist; that function has been defined as the power to "enlarge the borders of consciousness." He does it by showing us beauty and significance where we never suspected that such qualities existed.

A quick glance through the photographs in this section will reveal how well the camera can perform this service for us. It provides us not only with what has been happily termed a "frozen memory," but also with a glimpse of things which our own eyes cannot perceive. Take for example the picture on page 28. There, a brawny Highlander is swinging a mighty hammer preparatory to making his throw. If we watched such an event we should see only a swirl of movement. Nothing would stand out—none of the rhythm, the poise, the sense of effort. But the camera, in a split-second click of its shutter, has captured a vivid moment by stilling that tumble of arms and kilts. The thrower's supreme effort is frozen into immobility and at our leisure we can observe all the grace and energy in his pose.

It is worth noting also how the photographer exploits his camera to concentrate our attention on what is important. He eliminates his backgrounds, which otherwise might distract us from the foreground figure,

"AM I CLEAN YET?"

by W. SUSCHITZKY

THROW NET

by M. ARTHUR ROBINSON

by throwing them out of focus. They become merely a soft blur which frames but does not compete with the main interest of the scene. Notice the result on page 28.

The advent of the candid camera put into the hands of the best photographers a means of realising more nearly the aims which they had been striving for since they began to take their profession really seriously. It enabled them, that is to say, to go out and record aspects of life around them that they could not attempt before. It enabled them at last to perform that task which has been defined by one of the greatest of living camera artists to be the first and foremost duty of a photographer, the task, namely, of catching the eye and holding it. It brought life into photography and with it the insatiable interest of the world. It worked an artistic revolution that is comparable with any other in history.

Generally speaking, therefore, the candid camera has given photography the impetus to develop along one of its most significant courses, the depicting of incidents and character in life around us. It has done this with such striking success that it has gone a very long way to release the strangle-hold which the would-be "artistic" photograph (an abomination that was no more than a pale and lifeless imitation of paintings) was getting upon photography as a whole. The first essential of a good candid photograph is that it must be alive; composition, even technical competence are very secondary considerations, and are valueless if the first essential is absent.

From this it must not be deduced, as some people seem in danger of doing, that a good action picture must necessarily be of someone leaping into the air and grinning with delight. Excellent pictures of this type certainly are taken and can be seen in the following pages, but just as good or even better are those quieter studies, such as the one on page 75 of the old woman plodding along beside her donkey-cart. She is barely more than a silhouette against the road ahead, but the photograph has caught her just at the moment when her whole action and surroundings seem calculated to emphasise and force home to us the circumstances of her life and the tragedy that lies behind it. This is as true an action picture as any other in the book.

It is as well to correct another popular impression about action shots. The modern developments of high-speed lenses and films have enabled the camera to still the most impetuous movement. We have already noted one case (see page 28). In a later section (see "The Camera As Scientist") are many other action pictures that can truly be described as miraculous. But where studies of human interest are concerned such technical possibilities are often abused. The blurring which frequently results whenever photographs are taken of fast-moving objects is often an artistic aid. Action stilled to clear-cut immobility appears, in many cases, quite unreal, and the skilful photographer will remember this. Look at the picture "Where's That Ball?" on page 36. Neither the figure of the woman nor the figure of the dog is what photographers call *sharp;* their outlines are very slightly fuzzy. The effect is excellent, for it carries a suggestion of excited movement that would be lost were each figure clear-cut, sharply defined and utterly rigid. Part of the art of the photographer lies in knowing just how much sharpness to sacrifice to art.

The candid camera has, perhaps, secured its greatest triumph with stage photography—though its fullest possibilities have not yet been realised in that field. The forces of prejudice have been more difficult to overcome. The struggle here is between "stills" of scenes from the play, for which the actors pose on the stage—or sometimes by flashlight during a dress rehearsal—and shots taken with a miniature camera during an actual performance by ordinary stage lighting.

Studio studies of actors in character have been with us almost ever since the camera ceased to be a scientific marvel and became a commercial instrument. But modern camera art has worked a great revolution in the studio study. Those artificial, histrionic gestures, those wooden poses are things of yesterday. To-day the dramatic reveals itself in stark realism. The study of John Mills in the play *Of Mice and Men* (see page 17) has all the drama which one could desire. Here there is no actor in a play but a figure in reality.

It is interesting to compare such a study with an actual stage picture. Stage pictures are taken under the most exacting conditions and the photographer is compelled to work with the fastest possible film and the fastest possible lens. Miniature cameras are essential for this work, for no other camera combines such speed of lens with portability.

Unfortunately high-speed films do not lend themselves easily to enlargement free of graininess and blur; unfortunately, also, miniature camera negatives demand very great enlargement indeed if they are to compare with studio work. Even so, what the photographer can do is very impressive and it must be remembered that since his subjects are unconscious of his labour, his pictures have an unposed naturalness that studio studies often lack.

Magnificent examples of actual stage photography are to be seen on

JOHN MILLS IN ''OF MICE AND MEN''   **by BARON**

URGENT!   by **HOWARD COSTER**

pages 67 and 87. These studies of the ballet, action shots of surpassing grace and rhythm, yield nothing in beauty and design to those which the studio can give us.

The candid camera is not to-day concerned solely with individuals or single subjects; some of its greatest successes have been concerned with groups of people acting in crowds. It can and does catch and hold the fleeting moment in this connexion just as successfully as it can and does with the individual object. The remarkable back-view study of a seaside crowd on page 54, with its graceful suggestion of a formal painting, is a fine example of how the candid camera can capture beauty as well as record history. Mainly because of this development, it can safely be said that the work of the candid cameraman is going to be of the greatest possible historical importance. We have contemporary prints and portraits galore of the scenes and characters in the French Revolution, but what would we not give for a few photographs of that event and of the people who lived through it?

It can further be said that, in all probability, candid photographs will have a greater future than studio portraits. There are comparatively few people who to-day are interested in a photograph, however well taken, of you or me, unless we happen to be a Prime Minister, a Congress Leader, a "public enemy" or someone equally famous; there will be fewer still who will want to look at us 100 years from now. But a photograph of a crowd—perhaps containing you and me—cheering or taking part in a procession, or of a tragic incident such as an earthquake in Quetta, will be of enormous interest to millions of people and will, in the future, assume historical importance. Many of the photographs in the pictorial magazine of to-day have a world-wide value which will endure.

The relation between the candid camera and the age we live in is obvious to see. No longer can we sit at our ease dismissing such things as the slum problem with a few exclamations of polite horror and a transient feeling that "somebody ought to do something." Photographs now bring these things starkly to our notice with a vividness that refuses to be passed by. The picture of a slum on page 58 is evidence of this.

Such photographs are social documents which it is impossible not to read. They make us aware of the world around us and what is right and wrong with it, whether we like it or not. If it has done nothing else, the camera has made the pleading of ignorance—the ostrich-like burying of our heads in the sands of illusion—a very thin excuse..

FACES AT THE WINDOW   by **T. VECSENYI**

THE HORN PLAYER

by ROYE

FIDDLER

by JOHN EVERARD

A well-known London character whose monkeys and violin
have earned many a necessary copper from theatre queues.

2

CHESS PLAYER   by **F. GOLDRING**

THE CAMERA LOOKS AT US

A picture taken over thirty years ago on a Liverpool canal. The factory chimneys are now gone, but the barges, carrying the world's goods, still ply up and down the waterway and clouds of smoke and steam are still reflected in its placid surface.

SMOKE AND STEAM   by **THOMAS STEEL**

SKIPPER

by **W. E. BRIGGS**
Studio Briggs

"WHO'S THAT?"

PHOTOGRAPHER UNKNOWN
"A Kodak Snapshot"

THE CAMERA LOOKS AT US

An unconventional and unposed study, this photograph illustrates very clearly the full possibilities of the candid camera.

PORTRAIT UNAWARE

by HOWARD COSTER

THROWING THE HAMMER

by A. K. RITTENER
"A Kodak Snapshot"

A study in movement. The camera records for us a supreme moment of physical effort. The poise of the figure and amazing sense of rhythm could never be captured by the naked eye.

STRONG MAN   by **FRANK NEUBERT**

DISAPPOINTMENT

by OSCAR MARCUS

SATISFACTION   by OSCAR MARCUS

THE CAMERA LOOKS AT US

A study in light and shade of two men sleeping peacefully on a city bench in the midday sun. The position of the two figures and the unusual angle from which the photograph is taken, combine to make a striking and amusing composition.

LEISURE

by JOHN EVERARD

WORK

by E. G. BOON

Peasant women doing their household washing by the water-
side and chattering happily among themselves, are a familiar
part of the Italian scene. Here the camera has caught one
eager gossip at the very climax of her enthralling story.

MIKITCH AND HIS SHADOW

by **RICHARD FUCHS**

HUMAN SPIDERS

by **JOHN HATLEM**

"WHERE'S THAT BALL?"   by T. B. WADDICOR

"HULLO!"

by W. K.
CHADBURN
(Courtesy I.O.M.
Publicity Board)

HOLIDAY SPIRITS   by KARL SCHENKER

MISS VIRGINIA LEIGH   by CECIL BEATON

ELIZABETH WONDERS   by R. DOUGLAS PAUL

THE CAMERA LOOKS AT US

THE SKI RUN   by ERNÖ VADAS

SURF RIDING   by M. ARTHUR ROBINSON

"WELL
TACKLED,
SIR!"

A photograph
that reveals how
well the camera
can capture the
split-second
action of a fast
moving game.

by
CHRISTOPHER
JOHN WARE

"NOBODY LOVES ME"   by W. SUSCHITZKY

THE CAMERA LOOKS AT US

"SOUR!"   by W. SUSCHITZKY

"RIDE A COCK HORSE"

by SHAW WILDMAN
"A Kodak Snapshot"

FIRST ASCENT   by ERNÖ VADAS

WATER GYPSY

by CYRIL ARAPOFF

The camera catches a characteristic pose of an old woman who has lived on a barge at Leighton Buzzard, England, for many years. Bargees are almost a race apart and the waterways hold such a fascination for them that few water gypsies would desert their barge for the most luxurious life ashore.

LUNCH TIME   by ROYE

HANDS TO THE WHEEL

by ERNÖ VADAS

THE WATER DRINKER   by LEO A. LEIGH

The sense of space suggested by the immensities of sea and
sky is made more effective by the solitary foreground figure.

OLD MAN BY THE SEA

by ZOMER

BETWEEN THE LIVING AND THE DEAD   **by CHALONER WOODS**

The living soldier of to-day says good-bye to his girl in the
shadow of the memorial to the dead soldiers of yesterday.

BLACK BOY EATING SUGAR CANE   by M. ARTHUR ROBINSON

Acquisition

Experiment

Consideration

Satisfaction

HISTORY OF A BAR OF CHOCOLATE

by J. G. COWLEY

SEASIDE CROWD   **by JAMES MAYCOCK**

THE UNGENTLE SHEPHERDESS   **by R. SPELLAR**

A scene at the edge of the Serpentine in Hyde Park, London.

THE CAMERA LOOKS AT US

"WHAT HAVE YOU GOT?" by JULIUS ARNFELD

"A HUNTING WE WILL GO"

LONDON SLUM

by EDITH TUDOR HART

The dramatic squalor of the scene is greatly emphasised by
the unusual angle from which the picture has been taken.

THE AGITATOR

by E. M. HEDDENHAUSEN

HANDS AT WORK   by JOHN COLE

Selection of subject matter and an unusual viewpoint combine
in this study to produce a striking sense of vigorous effort.

THE DESIGNER

by **BARON**

WORK IN PROGRESS

The silhouette of
the crane hook and
the taut rope cuts
effectively across
the wide expanse
of earth and sky.

by **G. V. HERBERT**

THE CAMERA LOOKS AT US

THE SWIMMER

by FRANK NEUBERT

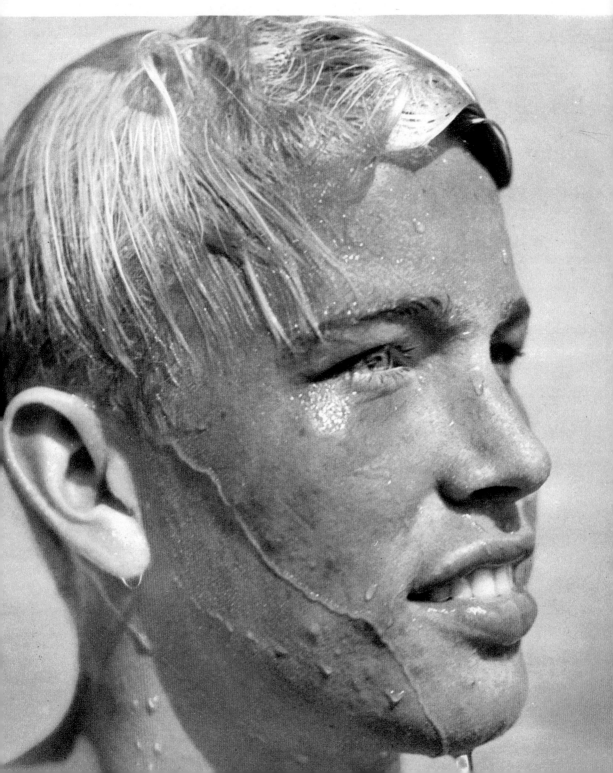

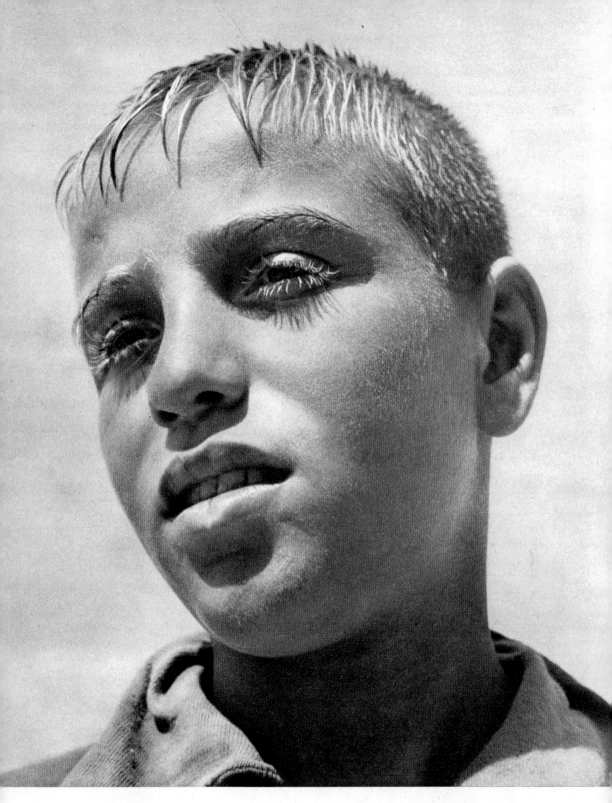

HEAD OF A YOUNG BOY   by **MARCEL GAUTHEROT**

Skilful use of lighting transforms what might otherwise have
been a humdrum scene into an arresting, dramatic picture.

THE MEAT CARRIER

by BRASSAI

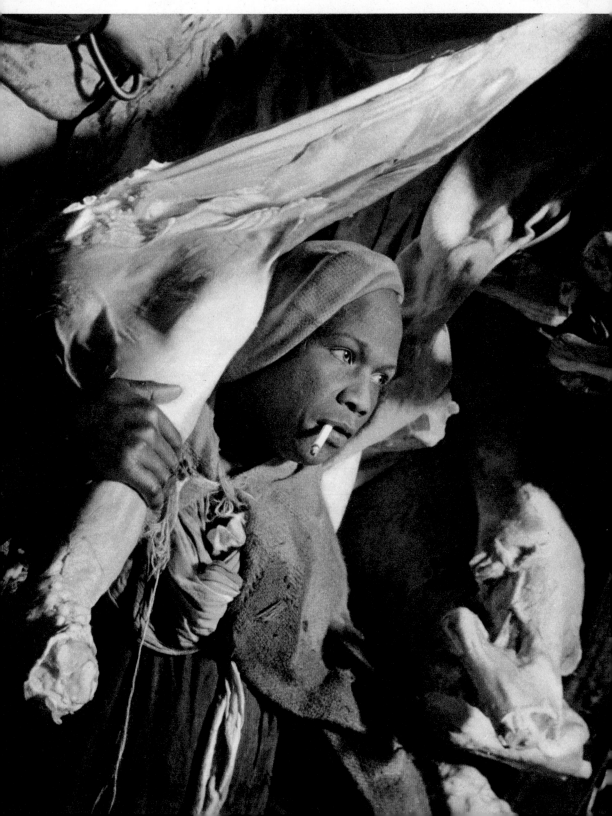

MLLE. BARONOVA   by **CECIL BEATON**

A lovely study in light and shade of Mlle. Baronova, the
famous ballet dancer, as she stands in the wings of the theatre.

"AWAY FROM IT ALL"   **by GABOR DENES**

An unusual character study of a small boy in an empty street
lost to the everyday world in the pages of his story book.

MARGOT FONTEYN   by BARON

Famous ballerina of the Vic-Wells Ballet, London.

A spectacular moment in the arena when the bull has jumped the barricade, driving the amateur bull-fighters into the ring.

INCIDENT IN THE BULL-RING

by ROYE

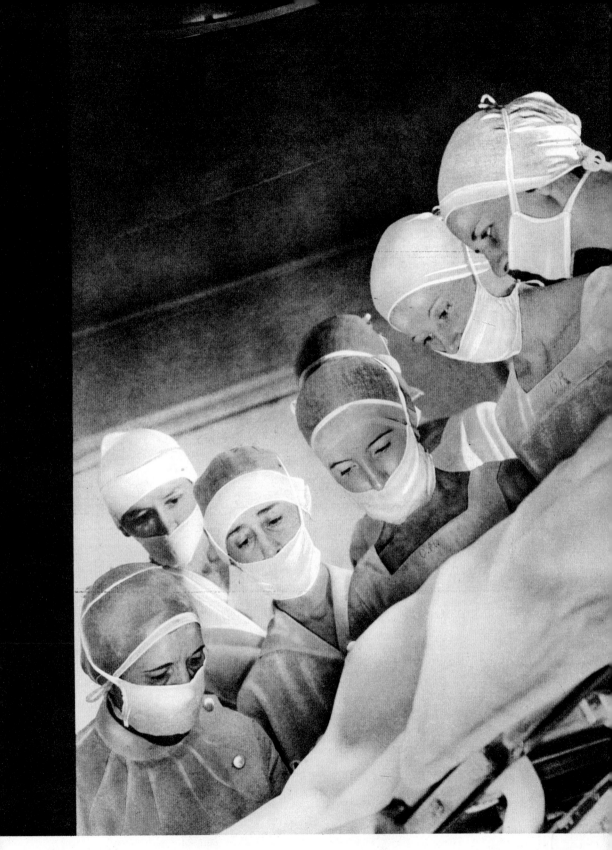

WOMEN IN WHITE

by **MAX THOREK**

THE LAUGHING LADY

by KURT LUBINSKI

THE BASKET WEAVER   by LEO A. LEIGH

ENGLISH ALLEY

by W. SUSCHITZKY

HUNGARIAN CAFÉ   by JOHN GABRIEL

A familiar scene in any Central European town are the little street corner cafés where the local notability gather to play cards with their neighbours. Here such a scene has been transformed into a striking and dramatic picture by accentuation of the shadows and high lights on the wall of the cafe.

THE CAMERA LOOKS AT US

Another picture with a moral. Careful lighting and positioning of the figures builds up a most striking contrast between the riches of the wax models and the poverty of the human being.

"BUY A FLOWER, LADY?"   by ROYE

WOMAN AND DONKEY   by ROYE

HOME FROM SEA   by **YATES MASON**

THE
WATER IMP

by
KAREL HAJE

THE CAMERA LOOKS AT US

The vast steel wall of the liner dwarfs the tiny rowing skiff and
its rower. White and black are combined in a striking pattern.

DAVID AND GOLIATH

by A. ELFER
(Courtesy of Italian Lines)

BALLET PATTERN

by CECIL BEATON

CHARWOMAN

by ROYE

WARMTH OF THE WINTER SUN   by FRANK R. FRAPRIE

BY THE OLD MILL

by **LEONARD MISONNE**

CORSICAN
GRANNY

The camera here catches perfectly the fat contentment of
the child, and by skilful use
of shadow emphasises the
smiling pride on the weather-
beaten face of the old woman.

by **ANDRÉ DE
DIENES**

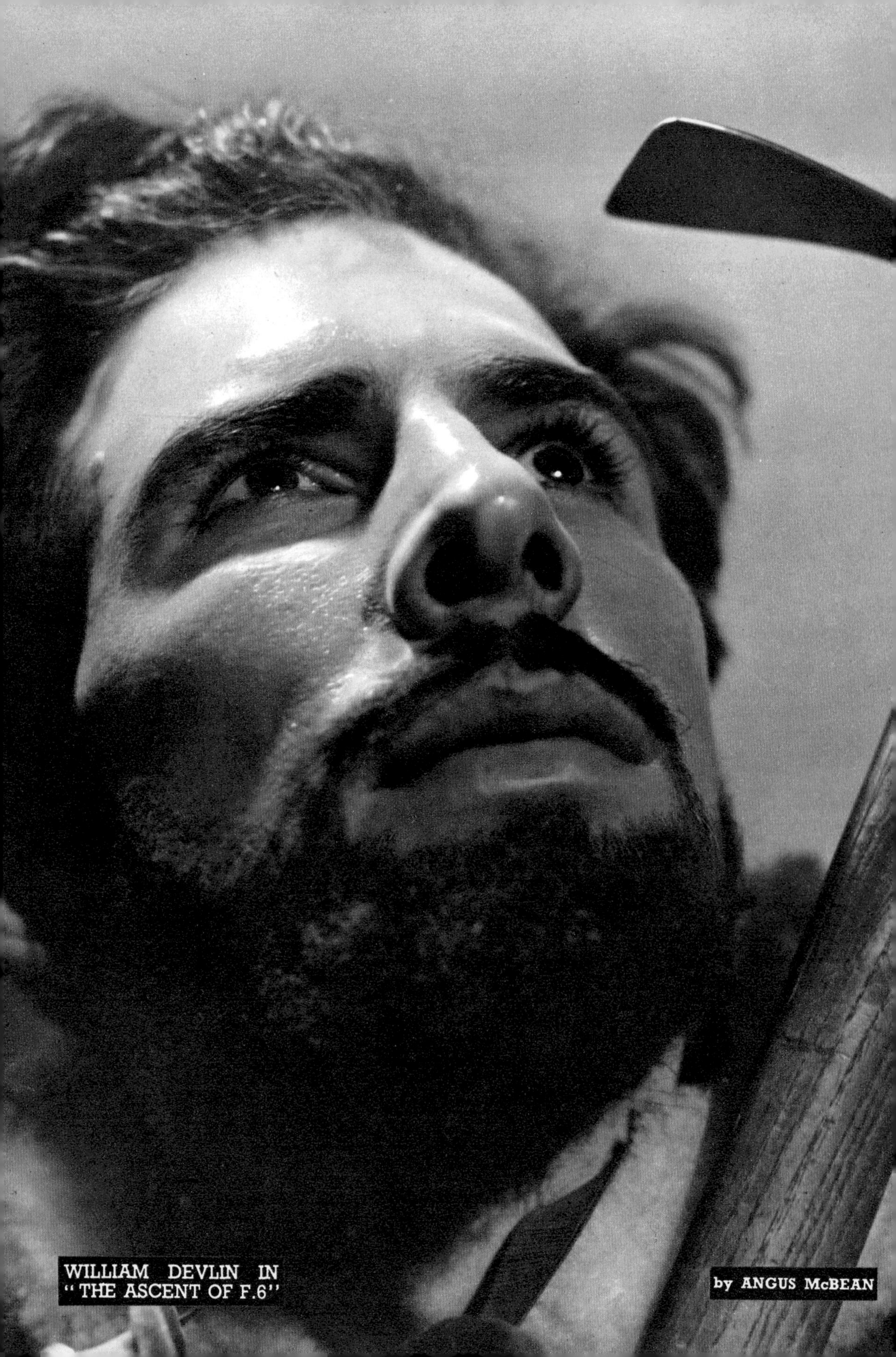

WILLIAM DEVLIN IN
"THE ASCENT OF F.6"

by ANGUS McBEAN

The shawl, framing this face, is skilfully used to focus attention on the hair and features and to emphasize the sorrow in the eyes.

STUDY IN SADNESS

by OTTO ILLAUER

AGE LISTENS   by **MAX THOREK**

YOUTH WORKS   by **MAX THOREK**

CLAY AND THE LIVING FLESH

by HANS STEINER

POETRY OF MOTION   by MERLYN SEVERN

SNOW, SKI AND HUSKY   by **BARON**

THE PAVEMENT BELOW   by **IMRE KINSZKI**

SHADOWS ON THE WALL

by **G. ROSSMANITH**
Gevaert Panchromosa Roll-film

The contrast between light and shade is here brilliantly depicted. Particularly pleasing is the deeper shadow of the woman which is seen reflected on the lighter shadowed wall.

WORK AMONG THE RAFTERS

by JOHN COLE

UNDERGROUND

by LEO. A. LEIGH

PHOTOGRAPHER AT WORK

by J. H. WILLINK
(Studio Sun)

ONE CAT IN THE SUN   by YATES MASON

THE CAMERA GOES HUNTING

In this section will be found a representative number of photographs of animals, birds, insects and fish. They range over all types of subject from the domestic cat to the wild zebra in its native haunts. Preference has been given to photographs of artistic worth, rather than to those of news or story interest only.

MANY psychologists maintain that the instinct to hunt is one of the most fundamental and powerful of all our instincts. Perhaps that is why those people who can afford it, whether they live in the East or the West, will spend large sums of money in organising elaborate expeditions to hunt animals of all sizes between elephants and foxes.

As the result of these expeditions, expeditions frequently involving much danger and hardship, the walls and floors of many of our larger houses bear upon them the skins and heads of countless animals. We cannot doubt that the killing of these animals delighted the hunters, but many of us doubt whether their stuffed bodies delight the beholders.

For this reason, if for no other, the advent of the camera is to be welcomed. It has presented the hunter with a new sport, a sport not of killing, but of recording. Those who value the dangers and hardships of the hunting expedition above anything else, lose nothing, for the modern cameraman, endeavouring to secure a photograph of a tigress nursing her cubs, is, if anything, in greater danger than the modern huntsman who, from his safe perch in a tree, waits to shoot the tiger about to take the kid helplessly tethered at the bottom.

So far as results of the two methods of hunting are concerned, there can be little doubt which the world at large prefers. A tiger shot by a gun becomes a glassy-eyed monstrosity of interest only to the proud hunter and his immediate family. A tiger shot by the camera becomes a thing of universal interest, for its pictures delight and instruct all.

We can learn nothing of interest from the head of a dead animal except what the head of a dead animal looks like; but a photograph of zebras collected at a water-hole in their native surroundings (such as the photograph shown on pages 104-105) tells us a great deal about the zebra, besides providing us with a beautiful picture.

Take also the superb study of giraffe heads on page 102, superb because of the graceful curves of their long necks set off so effectively against the high branches of the trees and the background of the sky. Here is a photograph that brings home to us, as no dead giraffe ever could, how beautiful these animals may be.

This is but one, and by no means the most important, of the various aspects of animal photography. The camera can hunt not only after the elephant, but also after the spider in its web. Very many of its most successful efforts are achieved, for example, with domestic animals.

Because we have seen horse, cow, sheep, cat and dog in dull photographs without number, we need not suppose that such animals do not lend themselves to delightful pictures. A glance through this section of the book should be conclusive. Two examples alone need be mentioned : that of the head of a pony on page 112, and of a young cow on page 111.

Dogs, compared with other animals, do not, as a rule, photograph well. They are far too anxious to please, and as a result become almost as camera-conscious as human beings. They pose resolutely in front of the camera like well-meaning children, or what is worse, take such an intense interest in what is going on that it is impossible to detach their attention for a moment. Unless one can detach their attention there is no chance of securing a good picture. Dogs must therefore be taken when they are off their guard, like the charming study of a borzoi and her puppies on page 110, or, better still, in action, with a camera working at high speeds, to catch the full beauty of their movements, like the greyhound seen on page 110.

The proper photographing of cats has been much hampered by those who have tried to over-sentimentalise them. As a lyric writer has wittily observed of these photographers :

"Their idea of Art
Is a very young cat
Looking out of a very old boot."

Their efforts were abortive and are now very rightly forgotten. As an example of a good cat photograph of the modern type, take the picture of the kitten on page 107, which with the enquiring look on its face is as charming as any subject can be, but it is in no way sentimentalised.

Birds, fish and insects, lacking the endearing human qualities of other animals, lose much of their value to the photographer, although there are brilliant exceptions such as the photograph, included in this section, of a cockatoo looking quizzically down at us from its perch on page 113, or the proud swan with her family of cygnets on page 100.

ELK BATHING

by **JOHN HATLEM**

WINGS OF THE NORTH   by JOHN PETERSON

Generally, however, photographs of these subjects rely for their appeal entirely upon the beauty of action that they display. High-speed lenses and films have enabled us to catch the seagull on the wing—as for example, on page 96—and thus fully to appreciate for the first time its almost miraculous grace of movement. It is by giving us pictures of this sort that the camera can score, for with no other medium would such accuracy of recording be possible.

Fish are even more difficult to catch with the camera than with a rod and line, and although many photographs have been taken under water, they are not generally satisfactory except as scientific curiosities. The only way to photograph this type of subject is through the walls of an aquarium where the opportunities are necessarily limited; the results are, again, valuable as scientific records, but not often as pictures.

Here also, however, there are brilliant exceptions, as when the photographer is able to catch the wonderful texture of a fish's scales or the liquid movement of its fins as it glides among the weeds. An example is seen in the study on page 108.

Insect photographs, too, are more often than not of scientific rather than artistic interest. With all the goodwill in the world, most people cannot summon up much enthusiasm for photographs of black beetles and wood-lice and are tempted to dismiss the whole subject out of hand without considering the wonderful photographic possibilities of the butterfly. On page 115 there is an amazing series of photographs showing the various stages of a butterfly's emergence from its chrysalis. These photographs are excellent examples of the sort of photograph which, besides being of interest to the scientist, have sufficient pictorial interest to be appreciated by everyone.

Practically all animal photography is the product of comparatively recent years. In this branch more than in any other branch of photography it is necessary, because of the nature of the subjects, to be able to take photographs at high speeds and such photographs have only been made possible by the more modern types of cameras and films. Before the advent of these cameras and films, animals could, of course, be taken in repose and some excellent work of this kind was done, but, collectively, it was not fully comprehensive and lacked the amazing variety that photographers are able to produce to-day. We now possess "candid camera" pictures of animals to match those we already have of ourselves. The results, as the following pages show, are some of the most charming and interesting that the camera has ever achieved.

HUNGRY HIPPO

by **JULIUS ARNFELD**

BILL THE BULLDOG   by **WALTER BIRD**

SWAN FERRY   by ROYE

PELICAN PARADE

by **JULIUS ARNFELD**

NECKING PARTY   by W. SUSCHITZKY

"MR. CHAIRMAN, LADIES AND GENTLEMEN"

by A. MIDDLETON

"A Kodak Snapshot"

ZEBRA AND WILDEBEESTE
AT A WATER-HOLE

by P. W. WILLIS

1. First Approach

2. Love Duet

3. First Results

4. Family Group

FOUR STUDIES OF PENGUINS

by H. G. PONTING

These amusing pictures are part of a series taken by the late H. G. Ponting on the Scott Antarctic Expedition of 1912.

"WHERE'S THAT MOUSE?"   by W. SUSCHITZKY

ANGEL FISH

by W. S. PITT

A denizen native of the River Amazon in South America, this
fish was taken under water, swimming among the reeds.

BUTTERFLY AT REST

by **H. TOTT**

BORZOI BABIES   by JULIUS ARNFELD

GREYHOUND ON THE TRACK   by J. C. A. REDHEAD
                                                 "A Kodak Snapshot"

SURPRISE

by BRASSAI

The soft tones of the dramatic background set off most admirably the enquiring pose of this sturdy young animal.

WINDBLOWN

W. SUSCHITZKY

COCKATOO   by **WALTER BIRD**

ANTARCTIC SEAL AND YOUNG   by H. G. PONTING

BARNYARD BULLY

The camera has
skilfully recorded
in this close-up
the fierce pride of
the old cock as well
as the texture of
skin and plumage.

by DEWEY CLARK

1. Leaving the Chrysalis

2. Out in the open

3. Fully developed

THREE STAGES IN THE BIRTH OF A BUTTERFLY

by J. ALLAN CASH

CAUGHT IN THE ACT   by A. H. DURRANT

THE SCARAB'S TASK

by R. VAN OUDTSHOORN

A Dung-roller beetle handles a ball many times its own size.

INVITATION TO THE PARLOUR

The pattern of the gossamer web is emphasised by the gross spider busily repairing the centre.

by
JENÖ AJTAY-HEIM

LORD OF THE JUNGLE   by W. SUSCHITZKY

WATCHING THE WORLD GO BY   **by ERNÖ VADAS**

The photographer has made of the bars of the cage an arresting background to the delicately poised figure of the bird.

A QUAY IN AMSTERDAM   by W. SUSCHITZKY

THE CAMERA AS ARTIST

In this section are to be found photographs first and foremost of artistic interest. They range from formal portraiture to flower studies and photos of architectural subjects. Still life shots and those pattern photographs, so distinctively modern in conception, are also features of this section. In the latter class the camera, perhaps, excels itself as in no other branch of photography. Nudes, landscape work, night studies, photos of snow, fog, cloud, mist and rain will also be found in this section.

THE artistic possibilities of photography have been the subject of much argument. Not only have photographers fought against the prejudice of those who have strenuously denied that the camera had any artistic possibilities, but they have also quarrelled even more violently among themselves as to what the camera should do if it is to be taken seriously as an artist.

It is an extraordinary story that is wrapped up with the entire history of photography.

The first photographers were artists in the usual sense of the word, that is to say they were painters. One of the best of them, a Scotsman called David Octavius Hill, working in Edinburgh, photographed his subjects primarily to guide him in the painting of their portraits. He was an inferior artist, but a magnificent photographer, with the rather ironic result that to-day his name lives entirely through the photographs which he took to help him to paint pictures that are now completely forgotten.

While it was still an artist's hobby the camera flourished and produced some excellent pictures which gave promise of a brilliant and unclouded future, but before long people began to wake up to the fact that it also had immense commercial potentialities. Thus, in the middle of the last century, the professional photographer came into being.

From the first, photography as a business was very careful to preserve its artistic associations. Photographers worked in "studios," they wore the back velvet coats and knotted cravats of the traditional artist, their backgrounds were the heavy draperies found in the portraits of the period. The result was, of course, that all serious artists came to regard photography as a debased form of art unworthy of consideration, and in consequence, no reputable artist would have anything to do with it.

Despite this sentence of artistic outlawry photography as a business prospered exceedingly. Not content with mere draperies as backgrounds photographers started using painted scenes to suit the temperament of the sitter. You could be photographed in a realistic-looking woodland glade, or sitting on a stile in the middle of a painted field, or even (and this was particularly popular) on the sea shore with mountainous waves breaking a few inches behind you. True, the head of the unfortunate sitter had to be clamped in a sort of vice in order to keep him still during the long exposures necessary (with the result that he nearly always appeared with a strained, hunted expression) yet the results pleased everyone concerned enormously and the demands to have "likenesses" taken steadily increased.

The discovery of the dry plate process towards the end of the century simplified *outdoor* photography enormously. Nevertheless in this, as in all other branches, photographers were continually hampered by the tradition that the ultimate aim of all their efforts was to produce photographs looking as near as possible like drawings and paintings—and if their results did not approach that ideal they were not considered "artistic."

During this period, which lasted into the "twenties" of the present century, some good work was certainly produced, notably that of the late Herbert G. Ponting, some of whose photographs, notably those taken on Captain Scott's Antarctic expedition in 1911-12, have, in their line, never been bettered. Two of these are seen on pages 143 and 212, but work of this kind was an infinitesimal proportion of the general output. Generally speaking, the standard of work, though technically excellent, was from the artistic point of view deplorable. The harder photographers worked for artistic effects, the more their object was defeated.

It was not, in fact, really until after the war that the modern movement in photography began to show itself. It began, in America, with a small group of men, artists in the true sense of the word, who realised that photography as a medium of expression should not be bound down by the traditions and conventions that applied to drawing and painting, that it must free itself from these and develop along its own lines. They experimented with the camera, taking everything regardless of whether it was generally regarded as "beautiful" or "picturesque," often from

FLOODLIGHT ON BIG BEN   by ALFRED CRASKE

THE CAMERA AS ARTIST

DANCING TORSO

by **WALTER BIRD**

extraordinary angles and with unusual lighting effects, and with results that breathed new life into photography which before had looked as though it were doomed, through a surfeit of bad art, to a dreary death among the dust and draperies of the old-fashioned photographer's studio.

It is, perhaps, not out of place to examine here the grounds for regarding photography as something essentially different from drawing and painting.

It is undoubtedly true that the camera can be made to lie, but generally speaking all photographs must have had for their subject something that actually existed. It is this fact that gives photographs that urgency and feeling of actuality that is their chief appeal. They represent reality caught in a fraction of a second of time and set down accurately before us to instruct, amuse, horrify, or what you will ; whether it be a picture of a famous politician or of a crankshaft, we know that each actually existed, at the time the photograph was taken, as we see them before us.

In this fact is to be found the essential difference between a photograph and a drawing. Whereas the latter must always be a very personal record of the impression the subject has made in the artist's mind, the accuracy or inaccuracy of which does not, from the artistic point of view, really matter, a photograph once it ceases to be accurate loses its value.

People may say, however: "Granted that a photograph is a completely different thing from a drawing, by what standards, then, can it be judged? If we are not to criticise photography from the same standpoint as the other graphic arts how are we to tell a good photograph from a bad one?"

To answer this it is necessary to have a clear idea of what you mean by a "good" photograph, a much more difficult thing to decide than what you mean by a "good" drawing. How can we say, for instance, whether a technically perfect photograph of the Taj Mahal is better than an equally technically perfect photograph of a jelly-fish in an aquarium? The answer does not really depend on whether you prefer architecture to jelly-fish, but on what the photographer has done with his subject in each case. Actually the chances are that the latter will win the prize. The beauties of architecture are familiar to most of us; hence, unless the photographer can throw some new light on this rather hackneyed subject his work will be merely commonplace. On the other hand the man who can produce an interesting, significant study of a jelly-fish has, in this hypothetical case, enlarged the borders of our appreciation by showing us beauty and significance in a subject in which we do not usually expect to find these qualities.

It is for this reason that pictures of such things as beautiful buildings, pretty girls, etc., have not found their way into this book unless they have some quality about them that gives them some interest beyond that of being mere representations of their subject. It may be that the ones included in this section have been taken from some unusual angle, like those on pages 123 and 140, both of which bring out so strikingly the essential grandeur of their subjects or that they show particularly beautiful lighting effects like the nudes on pages 153 and 172 or that they have caught some glorious natural effect like the waving corn against the cloud-flecked sky on page 148.

Perhaps even more interesting, however, as photographs are the studies of things which are apt to be overlooked by most people, such as the close-up of the line of foam on the sea shore which appears on page 181 or the pattern made by the shadows in the picture on page 244.

Portraiture also comes into this section, and in this line the artistic possibilities of the camera come increasingly to the fore. To take a good portrait the photographer must study the personality as well as the features of his sitter so that by lighting, pose and surroundings he can emphasise their essential characteristics. If the result is a success it will tell you more about the subject than pages of description.

It is impossible to dismiss this subject without some mention of Cecil Beaton whose work in the last fifteen years has revolutionised our ideas of photographic portraiture. To him more than to anyone else goes the credit for having successfully broken away from the old ideas upon studio portraits. Several examples of his work are to be found in this section of the book. The way in which he studies his subjects' personalities is to be seen very clearly, for example, in his portraits of M. Chirico and of Miss Marlene Dietrich on pages 156 and 157 respectively.

How then, we can now ask, can we discover if a photograph is a good one? The only safe method is to ask oneself three questions about it.

1. What has the photographer set out to do?
2. Was it worth doing?
3. How far has he succeeded in doing it?

It is on the answers to these three questions that one's final judgment on the photograph under discussion must depend.

H.R.H. THE DUCHESS OF KENT   by CECIL BEATON

WHITE HORSE INN

by **GEORGE GRABNER**

The ivy-clad wall and the inn sign on the right of the picture have been skilfully used by the photographer as a frame for the peaceful lakeside beauty of St. Wolfgang in Austria.

THE CAMERA AS ARTIST

STARK SENTINEL   by J. G. COWLEY

THE CAMERA AS ARTIST

STORM OVER ROME   by DONALD McLEISH

PILLARS AND SPIRE

by GISELA MARKHAM

The deep shadow on the foreground pillars of the National Gallery heightens the sunlight effect on the colonnade and on the neighbouring church of St. Martin-in-the-Fields, London.

SNOW, SHADOW AND SUNSHINE   by J. W. MATTINSON

PLOUGH ON THE SKYLINE   by **HAROLD BURDEKIN**

GINGER AND WALNUTS

by **CHALONER WOODS**

GRAPES IN A GLASS

by NOEL GRIGG
(Studio Briggs)

35

SUNSET IN THE SOUTH SEAS

by M. ARTHUR ROBINSON

THE CAMERA AS ARTIST

The great coils of rope form a snake-like pattern on the rugged stone-work of this fishing quay lit by the pale sunlight.

ROPE

by F. GOLDRING

WINDOW IN MARSEILLES   by **MARCEL BOVIS**

HERCULES

by **LEO A. LEIGH**

FLOWER IN THE WIND   by **PIERRE-ADAM**

THE CAMERA AS ARTIST

LOCH FYNE FROM INVERARAY

by R. DOUGLAS PAUL

MIGHTY MOUNTAIN

by H. G. PONTING

The contrast between the vast Matterhorn and the tiny house at the foot, the frame of the foreground fir-trees and the effect of the ground falling endlessly away, gained by taking the photograph from across a valley, should all be noted.

THE CAMERA AS ARTIST

PORTRAIT OF MISS KATHARINE HEPBURN

by CECIL BEATON

GEORGE BERNARD SHAW   **by MARCEL STERNBERGER**

An unconventional study of the playwright as philatelist.

POISED HEAD

by YATES MASON

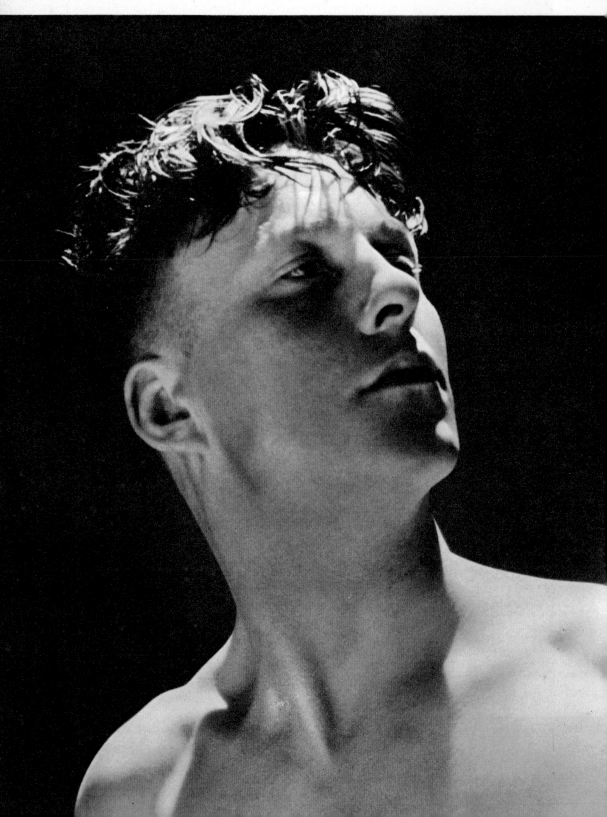

OVER HER SHOULDER   by R. DOUGLAS PAUL

RIPENING CORN

by F. GOLDRING

SKYSCRAPER   by EDWARD ALENIUS

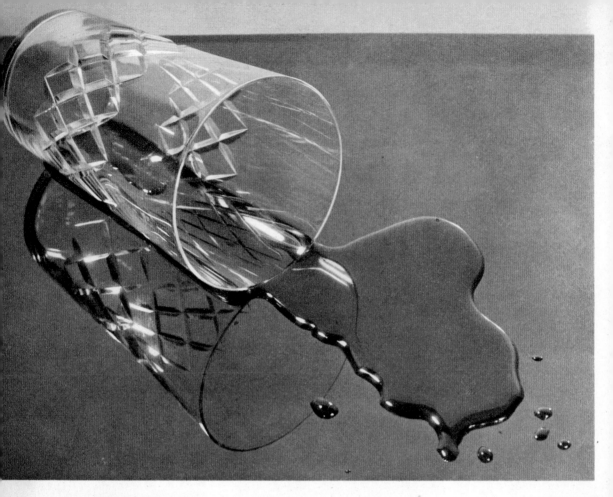

A GLASS UPSET   by S. SANDELL

RIPPLES IN THE SAND

The camera has caught the beauty of the light reflected from this strange sand formation frequently to be seen at low-tide on the North Sea coast of Germany.

by A. EHRHARDT

INDIAN VIEW

by EUSTON SEALY

ATHLETE OF MARTINIQUE   by PIERRE-ADAM

THE CAMERA AS ARTIST

An astonishing effect of shadow pattern on the body of a young girl, which gives almost the semblance of a summer dress.

STUDY IN SHADOWS

by W. SUSCHITZKY

ADELPHI ARCHES, LONDON　　　　　　　　　**by HUBERT DAVEY**

INTO THE
SUNLIGHT

**by
ANTE
KORNIČ**

ILLUSION

by G. MOUNIER

PORTRAIT OF M. CHIRICO   by CECIL BEATON

Chirico is one of the best known modern French Painters.

MISS MARLENE DIETRICH by **CECIL BEATON**

LEGS UNDER WATER   by **TIBOR CSÖRGEÖ**

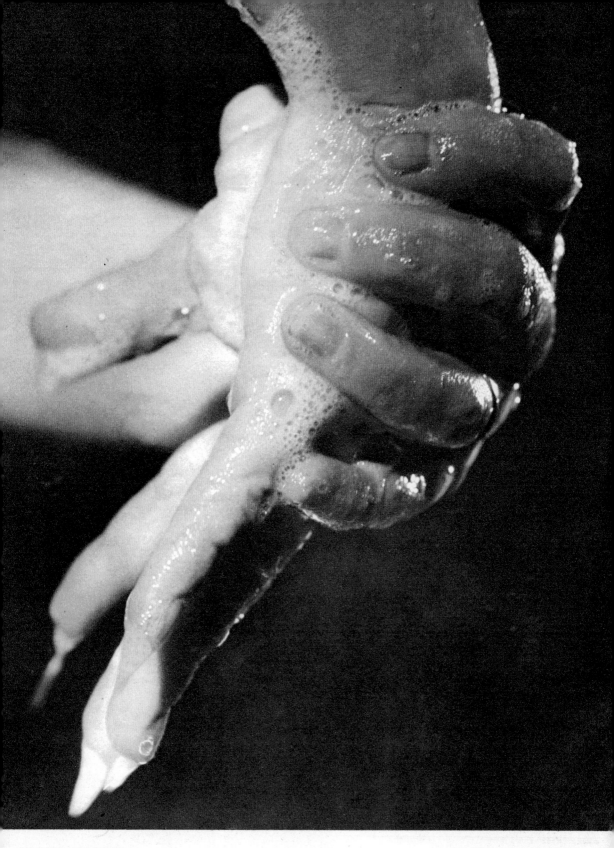

SOAPY FINGERS   by JAMES MAYCOCK

NEW YORK BY NIGHT   by PAUL J. WOOLF

THE CAMERA AS ARTIST

A complete contrast to the previous picture of a city's lights is the peaceful loneliness of this sky and mountain vista, which is made quietly sombre by the heavy foreground shadow.

MACKEREL SKY

by E. MEERKÄMPER
Gevaert Panchromoso Rollfilm

NICOLAS NABOKOFF

by CECIL BEATON

OLIVER MESSEL

by **PAUL TANQUERAY**

VIEW OF THE PARTHENON   by **MARCEL GAUTHEROT**

The much-photographed Parthenon in the Acropolis at Athens
gains in interest by being framed between these two pillars.

TEMPLE IN MYSORE   by FRITZ HENLE

SKI-TRACKS IN THE SNOW

by **ROSEMARY GILLIAT**

Figures of unnatural blackness against the dazzling whiteness
of the snow, a party plods upwards to higher ski-ing slopes.

BY THE LAKESIDE   by **EDWIN BROOMER**

RURAL ENGLAND   by **R. SLEEP**

OUT OF THE WIND   by G. G.

FLOWER STUDY

by GORDON CROCKER
(Studio Sun)

The dramatic use made in this photograph of light and shade
is an admirable setting for the exotic nature of this orchid.

COLETTE

by CECIL BEATON

Portrait of a well-known French authoress.

THE CAMERA AS ARTIST

MISS LUISE RAINER

by **ANGUS McBEAN**

STUDY IN THE NUDE   **by JOHN EVERARD**

Great skill in lighting gives the flesh of this young girl almost
the look of alabaster, and the features are subtly underlined.

MERMAID by **ROYE**

GEFION FOUNTAIN, COPENHAGEN   by E. HEIMANN

PEARL MOSQUE, AGRA   by FRITZ HENLE

CLOVER-LEAF CROSSING, NEW YORK   by **PAUL J. WOOLF**

MISS GLORIA SWANSON   by **CECIL BEATON**

WAITING SHADOWS

by F. P. TAYLOR

The eye is here made to follow these shadows to their sources,
the waiting passengers whose feet can be seen on the left.

THE CAMERA AS ARTIST

REFLECTIONS IN AMSTERDAM by W. SUSCHITZKY

ST. PAUL'S BY FLOODLIGHT by **HUBERT DAVEY**

GOSSIP IN MIDDLEBURG, HOLLAND

by DONALD McLEISH

"AT THE GOING DOWN OF THE SUN"

by G. ROSSMANITH
"A Kodak Snapshot"

FOAM PATTERN   by A. EHRHARDT

THE CAMERA AS ARTIST

"PRETTY POND LILY"

by F. GOLDRING

NIGHT ON THE EMBANKMENT   by HAROLD BURDEKIN

BEACHY HEAD

by J. TOFT BATE

THE EDGE OF THE LAKE
by JOHN ERITH

SAFETY

by HAROLD BURDEKIN

FOOTPRINTS IN THE SAND   by F. GOLDRING

BEAUTY AND BRACKEN   **by ROYE**

THE CAMERA AS ARTIST

"SHOWERS LOCALLY"

by F. GOLDRING

VILLA ROTONDA VICENZA

by A. COSTA

An unusual photograph which perfectly catches the elaborate
detail of this superb example of Italian baroque architecture.

THE WOOL MARKET   by BERNARD ALFIERI

The famous wool market at Chipping Campden, England

THE CAMERA AS ARTIST

by W. SUSCHITZKY

REPOSE

by ANGUS McBEAN

The striking pose of the man's body is outlined by deep shadow
and the living flesh contrasts with the bare boards beneath him.

SLEEPING WOMAN   by ROYE

THE CAMERA AS ARTIST

MEADOW IN MIDSUMMER

by **WALTER BIRD**

FROM A CITY ROOF-TOP   by P. DUBREUIL

SUNLIGHT IN THE SUBWAY

by S. HEDGELAND

A simple yet striking study in light and shade taken from near
the entrance to a subway in a London Underground Station.

THE CAMERA AS ARTIST

A BREAK IN THE CLOUDS   by H. A. MURCH

NIGHT EXPRESS

by HAROLD BURDEKIN

EGGS   by F. **GOLDRING**

PRECISION

by R. N.
CRAIGEN
(Studio Briggs:
Courtesy of
Henry Hughes
& Son Ltd.)

BROOMS FOR SALE

by E. G. BOON

THE CAMERA AS ARTIST

BALTIC SAND DUNES   by **A. EHRHARDT**

NIGHT IN SUBURBIA

by JOHN COLE

A street corner in any suburb on a wet night. The camera lends an air of beauty and mystery to an ordinarily drab subject.

WOMAN'S BACK

by **BRASSAI**

CINEMA ORGANIST   by **YATES MASON**

THE CAMERA AS ARTIST

The graceful pose of the woman's body, the subtle monotone of the whole picture and the unusual angle from which it has been taken combine to produce a vigorous air of realism.

FREEDOM

by CHALONER WOODS

HIGH LIGHTS AND SHADOW   by ROYE

PONT ST. MICHEL, PARIS

by PIERRE-ADAM

THE CAMERA AS ARTIST

A THAMES SUNSET   by DONALD McLEISH

MOUNT FUJIYAMA, JAPAN   by H. G. PONTING

AT THE
FOOT OF
MOUNT
SNOWDON

by F.
GOLDRING

VILLAGE IN THE VALLEY   by ROYE

EGYPTIAN TEMPLE

by DONALD McLEISH

THE CAMERA AS ARTIST

The old and the new are effectively mingled in this country house interior with its modern dining-room and old oak door.

by F. GOLDRING

THE SHADOW OF THE LAW

by JOHN H. AHERN

LAUNDRY SILHOUETTE   by JENÖ DENKSTEIN

STEP BY STEP   by F. S. LINCOLN

TIDE   by **WARD HUTCHINSON**

219

PONT DE LA TOURNELLE, PARIS

by PIERRE-AI

BARGES IN THE
DOCKS

An interesting examp
of how the camera c
find beauty in such cor
monplace surroundinc

by GABOR DENES

EW FROM ST. PAUL'S, LONDON   **by PAUL POPPER**

THE DODOS

An interesting example of composition in night photograp.
The brilliant lighting is provided by a single street lan

THE KING'S GATE, MARBLE ARCH — by **HAROLD BURDEKIN**

PORTRAIT IN PROFILE

by BARON

The use of deep shadow makes this study an arresting one.
Note also the half-light, emphasising the texture of the hair.

THE CAMERA AS ARTIST

WHITE DAHLIA   by G. MOUNIER

ST. PAUL'S FROM LUDGATE CIRCUS   by JACK DAVIS

LONELY ROAD   by **ROYE**

RUINS OF TIMGAD

by YVONNE CHEVALIER

SUNSHINE ON THE
PAVEMENT

Another example of how
the camera can make
striking a scene that holds
no very obvious beauty.

by SOUTHWELL EADES

THE CAMERA AS ARTIST

The stillness of a hot noonday in Southern France is strongly emphasised by the two figures picked out by the shaft of sunlight.

STREET IN ST. TROPEZ   by YATES MASON

PORTRAIT OF MISS CLAIRE LUCE   by CECIL BEATON

MOUNTAIN WALL   by H. A. MURCH

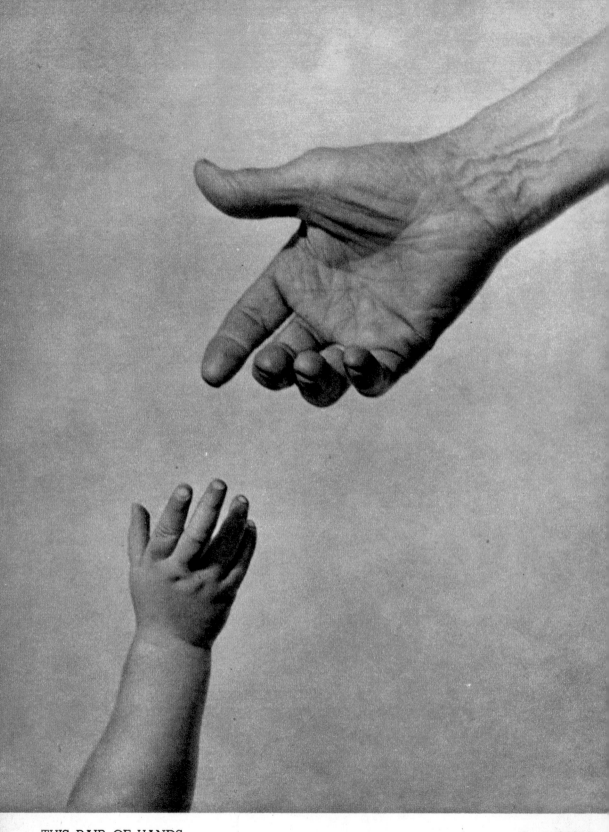

THIS PAIR OF HANDS by **T. BERRY**

FINGERS ON THE DRUM

by JAMES MAYCOCK

FOG AT SCOTLAND YARD

by B. SAIDMAN

The peculiar, sinister effect of the sunlight in the fog, contrasts
with the solidity of the London policeman impassively on duty

HALF CONQUERED BY THE WIND   by J. EATON

INTERIOR, CARLISLE CATHEDRAL

by W. ELLISON

VENETIAN STUDY

by H. TOTT

THE CAMERA AS ARTIST

This camera study of the Lake of Geneva at eventide is notable for its excellent composition. No landscape painter could arbitrarily have placed the various features to better advantage.

EVENING ON THE LAKE

by R. M. KIRKPATRICK

THE HEART OF THE COUNTRY

by **HUBERT DAVEY**
(Courtesy of Messrs. Worthington)

VIEW OF CALCUTTA

by **T. H. MAYNARD**

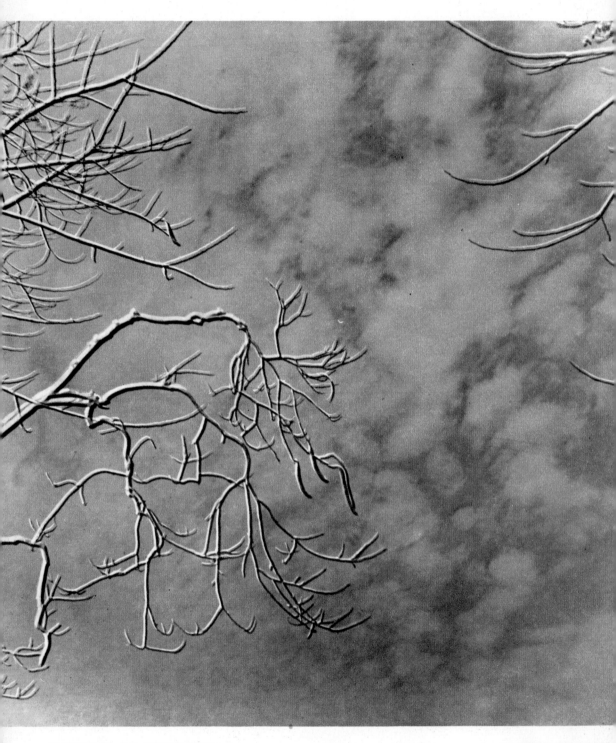

PATTERN OF BRANCHES

by EUSTON SEALY

Like the finest tracery work these leafless twigs form a picture
made more effective by the cold impersonal winter light.

INTERIOR DECORATION

by **SYDNEY K. MATTHEWS**
Courtesy of English
Speaking Union
Studio Sun

SHADOW PATTERN

by E. C. Le GRICE

APPLES

by **PIERRE AURADON**

SPIRAL STAIRCASE

Looking up the well of a stair-case in a large Paris apart-ment-house.

by **F. S. LINCOLN**

MOROCCAN SHADOW

by CECIL BEATON

A heavily shrouded native woman lends an air of mystery to
this picture which is further emphasised by the flecks of brilliant
sunlight. These combine to make this a superb photograph.

SNOW AND STEAM

by **JOHN GABRIEL**

LIGHTS OUT

An interesting picture of the curious pattern made by the smoke from a candle just after it has been blown out.

by **OTTO ILLAUER**

SKIS IN SINGLE FILE

by TIBOR CSÖRGEÖ

THE CAMERA AS ARTIST

The camera angle has in this photograph produced heavy elliptical shadows that bear in shape no apparent relation to the spectacles that have cast them, but form an interesting pattern.

SPECTACLE SHADOWS

by **P. DUBREUIL**

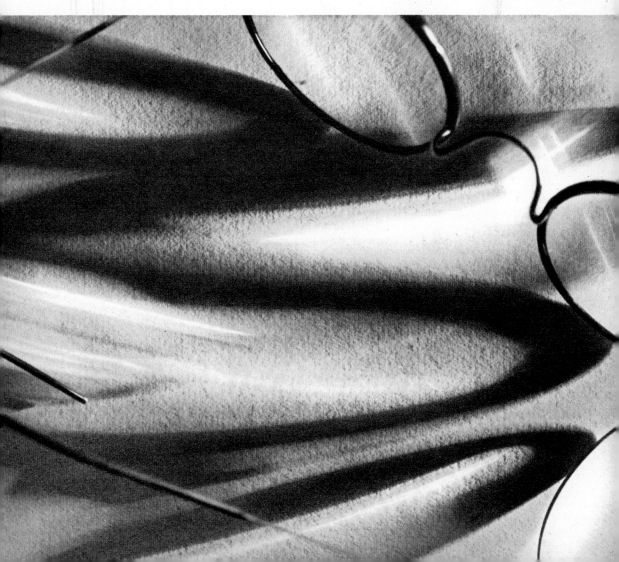

VIEW OF ST. MORITZ

by R. M. KIRKPATRICK

A TOWER IN FLORENCE   by FRITZ HENLE

THRESHOLD OF LIFE   by JAN LUKAS

Though beautifully posed, both subjects in this picture are unaware of the camera and so can be seen as they actually are.

FLOODLIGHT ON BATH ABBEY   by PAUL FRIPP

THE CAMERA AS ARTIST

SEARCHING THE SEA   **by A. COSTA**

Verging on the melodramatic, this photograph taken on the
Dalmatian coast at Dubrovnik shows what startling effects the
camera can achieve by the use of deep shadow and highlights.

THE CAMERA AS ARTIST

The filth and depression of a rainy day is epitomized in this study of blur and wet and a girl jumping over a puddle.

AVOIDING THE PUDDLES

by W. SUSCHITZKY

THE RINGBOLT   By EDWIN BROOMER

THUNDER IN THE AIR

by T. VECSÉNYI

PONT DES ARTS, PARIS

by PIERRE-ADAM

THE CAMERA AS ARTIST

The effect of suspended activity which so often obtains when the ground is mantled in snow, is reproduced in this photograph.

CHRISTMAS TREES

by TIBOR CSÖRGEÖ

A STREET IN THAW   by T. H. WOODWARD

THE SENTRY  by CHALONER WOODS

THE MILL   **by RONALD BEAUCHAMP**

Isolated in apparently deserted country, this Oxfordshire mill
stands as a reminder of the old days before machinery was used.

THE CAMERA AS ARTIST

TAIT'S TOWER, GLASGOW EXHIBITION   by J. G. COWLEY

A FRAMEWORK FOR NELSON

by W. SUSCHITSKY

By a trick of the camera it appears as if this lamp standard in Trafalgar Square was actually part of the Nelson monument.

WORKERS OF PARIS

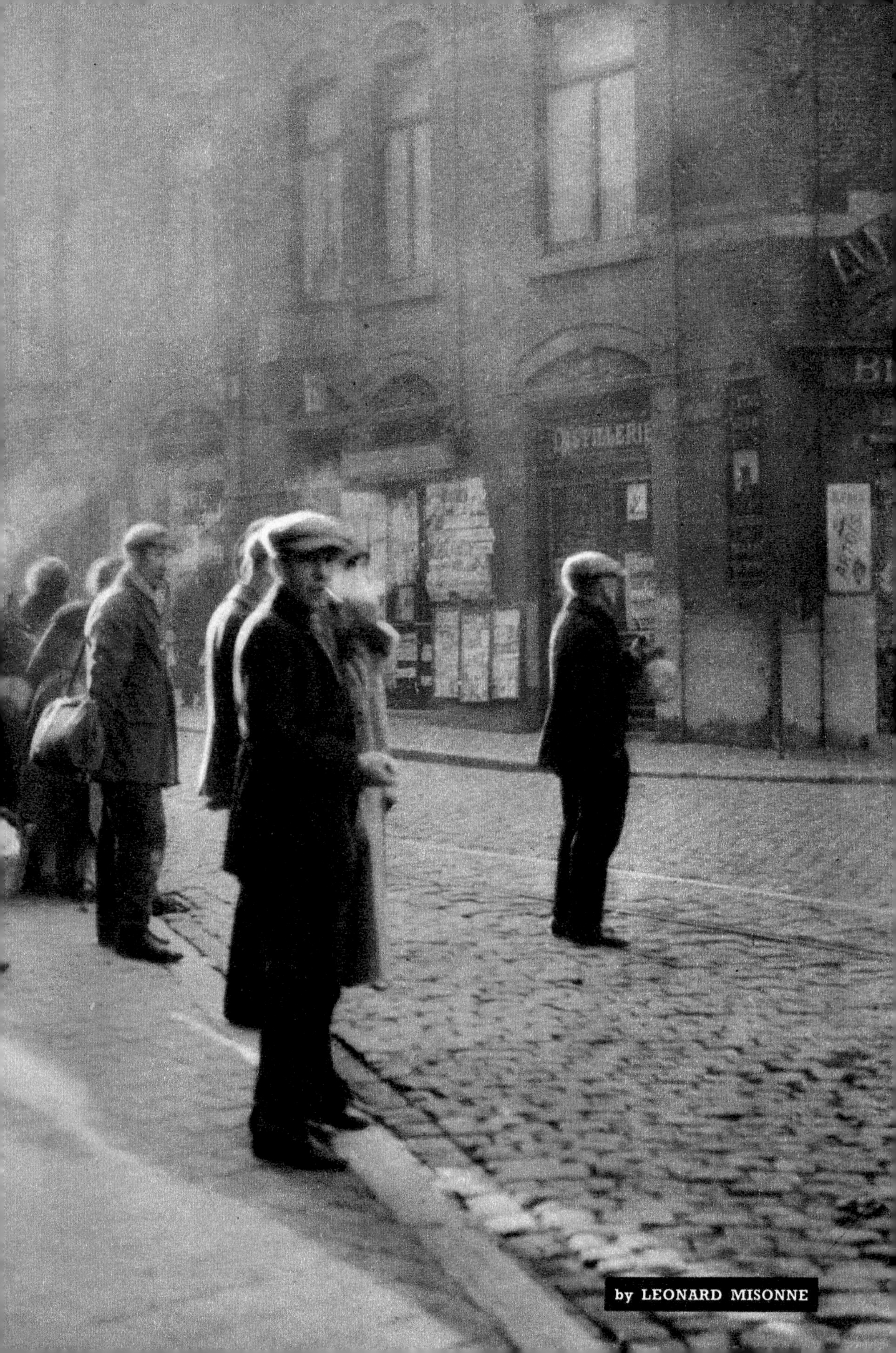

by LEONARD MISONNE

MOUNTAIN GLACIER by K. KOIKE

THE MOTOR AND THE MAN

by M. N. DU MONT

TUMBLE-DOWN HOUSE

The owner ponders at the steps to his house, the shabby nature of which is emphasized by the brilliant sun on the walls.

by QUINTO ALBICOCCO

STUDY OF A GIRL

by BRASSAI

YOUTH HAS ITS FLING   by B. KRÖHN

A remarkable action photograph, in which the camera has
arrested these girls at the maximum impetus of their leaps.

GLASS AND SHADOWS   by J. G. W. THOMPSON

The glass and bowl throw strange shadows, almost like an
X-ray photograph of a foot, with the bones showing up white.

NET BUOYS   by **D. V. T. TAYLOR**

CORKS AND SCREW

"Dead" corks lie in a heap,
around their "slayer,"
the corkscrew to produce
an unusual still life study.

by **P. DUBREUIL**

IN RURAL INDIA

by N. J. **NALAWALLA**

SUNLIT COLONNADE   by R. WAGSTAFF GIBBS

NEW YORK CONTRAST

by **BRUGUIERE**

THE CAMERA SHOWS ITS PACES

In this section will be found photographs demonstrating the scientific possibilities of the camera. They range from unusual angle shots through microscopic and X-ray studies to infra-red and high-speed photographs. Here also are to be seen experimental studies as well as the new art of photomontage—the building up of a composite photograph from a number of quite unrelated negatives.

IT always happens with any new discovery that it is not long before people try to make it play tricks. Usually the results are quite valueless and not particularly amusing, like playing a gramophone record backwards, but with photography the reverse has been the case. The more it is played with the more powers and wonders it displays.

Who, for instance, would have guessed what a beautiful pattern is made by the splash of a drop of milk unless a photographer, while trying out his high-speed camera, had recorded it for us as seen in the picture on page 285?

In this section of the book, therefore, are included examples of some of the more unusual things that the camera can do. Most of these examples are beautiful as well as curious. All of them are remarkable for their originality, and would have been incredible a few years ago. In recent times the camera has proved, as the following pages show, that it can, for instance, reveal to us the wonders of the world of science, like the picture of the air waves made by a bullet shown on page 289, or the amazingly beautiful pattern of the minute marine animals as seen through a microscope on page 296.

All this demonstrates very forcibly, the flexibility of photography as a medium of expression. It has the perverse but engaging quality of having practically no rules connected with it that cannot be broken with impunity. The more the pundits try to tie it down with principles of artistry or technique, the more it seems to delight in flouting them.

"Let's see what this girl looks like through some netting," says the photographer, and immediately sets out to show us, as in the example on page 277. It occurs to him when looking at a negative that the picture is more interesting that way, so he makes the print in reverse (page 297), or by another simple process he can caricature his subject in the extraordinary but extremely amusing way shown on page 282.

Another interesting trick that is only as old as photography itself, but that is extensively used to-day, is the process known as photomontage. This is the making of a composite photograph from several different negatives or mixing photographs and drawings. In its debased form this method is used deliberately to deceive, as is done continually in commercial studios where figures taken indoors by artificial lighting are attached to backgrounds showing some outdoor scene, usually with extremely unconvincing results. However, when the mixing is done artistically with no attempt at crude deception, striking compositions result.

Take, for instance, the picture on page 283, which by this montage method very plainly tells its story, or the unusual picture on page 278, a beautiful and arresting design which by the combination of various, apparently incongruous, subjects conveys an extraordinary feeling of space and vastness in a subtle manner worthy of the best artistic traditions.

Special processes are also represented here, such as infra-red photography, by which the camera is able to outdo the human eye in being able to see vast distances in spite of fog or mist, as in the examples on page 295, showing Mount Everest seen from a hundred miles away, and the whole of the Isle of Wight from the air.

So long, it seems, as photographers continue playing tricks with the camera, so long will they continue to obtain valuable results. Some of the tricks may, it is true, be valueless, and others merely irritating. Yet it is broadly true to say that each fresh trick marks a fresh advance in the camera's potentialities. The pictures in this section demonstrate forcibly that photography, whatever else it is, is not a static art. Constantly it is developing. The possibilities of infra-red photography, for instance, or of combining drawing with photography, are only just beginning to be realized. The potentialities of the former are fascinating. To be able to see—even if it is only at second-hand, over a distance of 100 miles or more, is a thing that only a few years ago would have been thought beyond the bounds of credulity or possibility. And in the latter field there is surely a chance for an original and creative mind to develop what would appear to be one of the most interesting branches of photography. So far only the fringes of the subject have really been touched.

In this, as in other experimental branches of photography, we may look forward to some surprising developments in the future—which fact alone would make photography a most enthralling subject for study.

PATTERN PORTRAIT

by MAN RAY
Courtesy of J. T. Soby

PHOTOMONTAGE

by BARBARA MORGAN

FISHERMAN'S DREAM

by **M. ARTHUR ROBINSON**

The photographs on this and the opposite page are striking examples of the camera-art of photomontage. Many negatives went to the making of each composition, and the final results convey their effects with astonishing power.

PAVILION AT THE PARIS EXHIBITION   by **WALTER BIRD**

An example of angle-shot photography in which the peculiar
foreshortening, due to tilting the camera, has been effectively
exploited. This study of modern architecture furnishes an
interesting contrast with that seen on the opposite page.

TOWER OF THE KUTB MINAR, DELHI   by FRITZ HENLE

THE CAMERA SHOWS ITS PACES

An example of caricature by photography

BORED BOY

by CHALONER WOODS

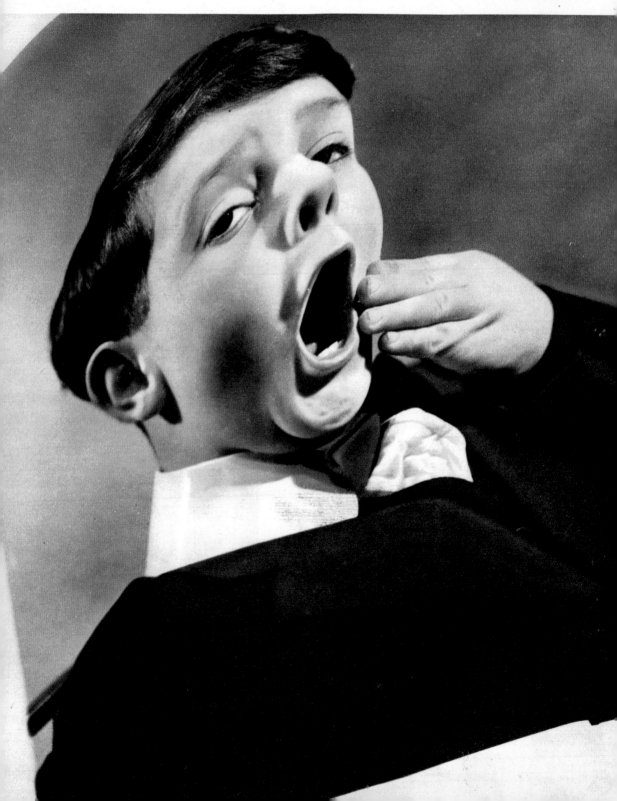

BEHIND THE HEADLINES   by **DONALD S. HERBERT**

A MILK JUG BREAKS

by **W. L. VINING**
Courtesy of the "Daily Mirror"

Specialised apparatus and spark photography have revealed, through the medium of the camera, details of events which otherwise could never have been studied. Above is seen a milk jug breaking into pieces as it hits the ground. On the opposite page is seen the beautiful corona set up by a drop of milk falling into a thin layer on a plate. The white blob at the top is a second drop falling. The latter photograph was taken at an exposure of 1/100,000th of a second.

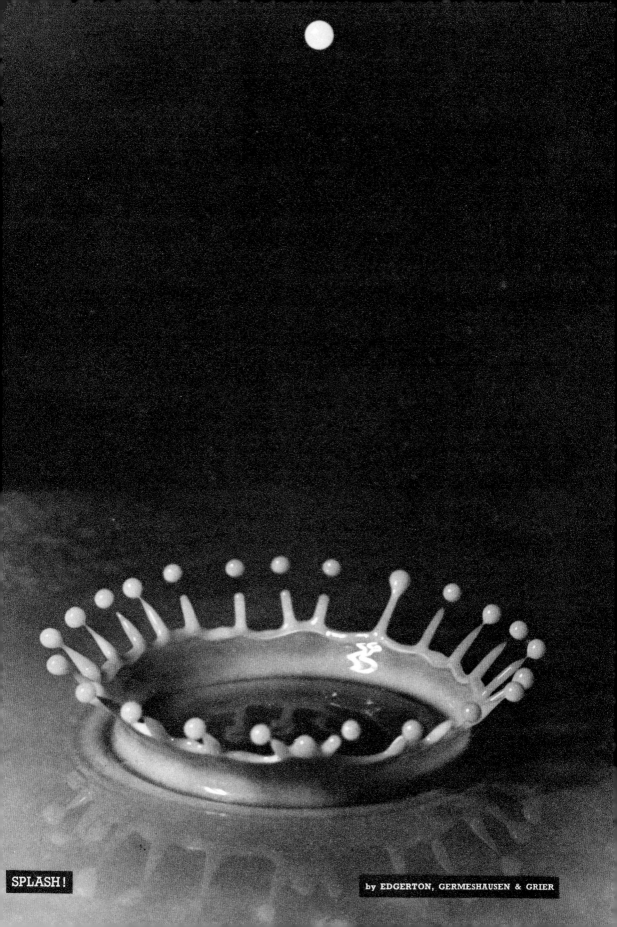

SPLASH!

by EDGERTON, GERMESHAUSEN & GRIER

SUNRISE   by G. AUBOURNE CLARKE

The camera has become of great use to meteorology in its
ability to record cloud formations. These two very beautiful
studies show (above) cloud layers illuminated by the sunrise,
and (below) masses of black and white thunder clouds.

THUNDER CLOUDS   by G. AUBOURNE CLARKE

FIREWORKS   by G. KARGUEL

287

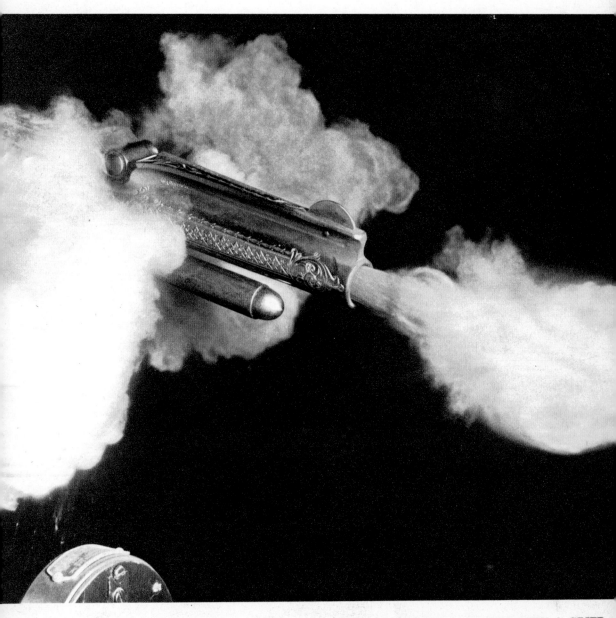

AN OLD REVOLVER FIRES by **EDGERTON, GERMESHAUSEN & GRIER**

Another striking example of high-speed photography. The bullet, just emerging from the muzzle, is obscured by the puff of gas that has leaked past. The photograph was taken with an exposure of nearly one millionth of a second.

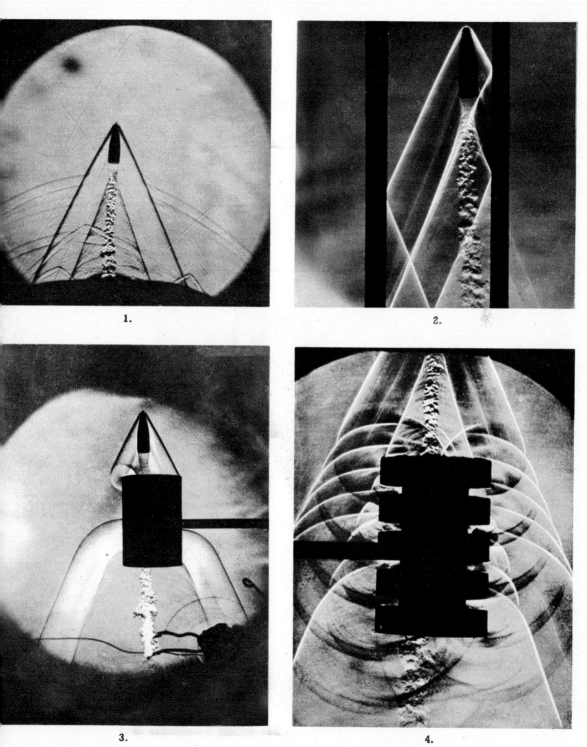

1.

2.

3.

4.

A BULLET IN FLIGHT

PHOTOGRAPHER UNKNOWN

Amazing shadow pictures showing the air waves round the projectile (1) when travelling free; (2) when shot between two plain metal plates; (3) through a plain tube; (4) through a perforated tube. Notice the wake travelling behind the bullet.

BOBBY JONES IN PLAY

PHOTOGRAPHER UNKNOWN
Courtesy of A. G. Spalding & Bros.

CLUB KALEIDOSCOPE

PHOTOGRAPHER UNKNOWN
Courtesy of A. G. Spalding & Bros.

On the opposite page a high-speed photograph (1/50,000th second) showing how a golf ball is squashed out of shape at the exact moment when it is hit by the club. Below is a multiple flash photograph, the exposure for each picture being 1/100,000 second with an interval of 1/100 second between each. From this photograph it was possible to calculate the speed of the ball as 225 feet per second and the club velocity as 166 feet per second before impact, and as 114 feet per second after impact.

THE CAMERA SHOWS ITS PACES

Unsuspected beauties revealed by this type of photography.

DAFFODILS BY X-RAY

by HERBERT FLOWER
Courtesy of Ilford Limited

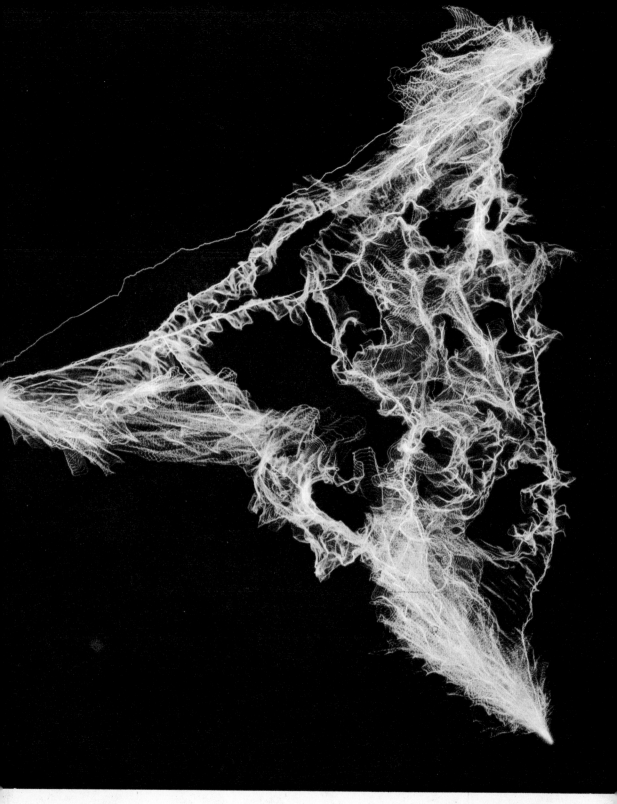

ELECTRIC LACE

by **ELLISON HAWKS**

This beautiful pattern was made by a 1,000,000-volt three-phase spark, and shows clearly how an electric current moves about seeking the path of least resistance through the air.

ILLUSION IN SIZES

by JOHN HATLEM

THE EVEREST RANGE

by THE HOUSTON-MT. EVEREST EXPEDITION
Courtesy of "The Times"

By the aid of infra-red photography we can "see" for immense distances. Above, taken at a height of 22,000 feet, the summits of the Mt. Everest range are seen from over 100 miles away. Below, the whole of the Isle of Wight, an area of 147 square miles, and even the French coast across the English Channel, are seen from a height of 15,000 feet.

THE ISLE OF WIGHT

by A STAFF REPORTER OF "THE TIMES"
Courtesy of Ilford Limited

WATER ON A LEAF   by **BRASSAI**

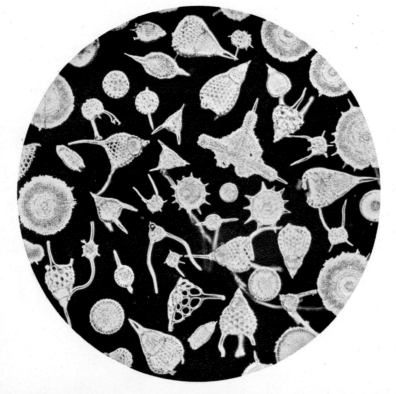

SEEN THROUGH THE
MICROSCOPE

A study of minute marine
animals known as Radiolaria.

by **RANALD RIGBY**

NEGATIVE PRINT   by **GISELA MARKHAM**

H.M.S. ''ROYAL OAK'' AT GIBRALTAR   **by YATES MASON**

THE CAMERA AFLOAT AND IN THE SKY

In this section will be found sea and sky photographs. The former range from studies of ships of all sizes to pictures of the sea in all its phases; the latter from studies of aeroplanes to aerial photographs of every description.

IF landscape photography is often disappointing in its results the balance is amply made up by the magnificent photographs that can be taken of the sea and all the fascinating things connected with it. Harbours, quays, ships, all have a picturesqueness about them and, at the same time, a feeling of vitality and life that make them ideal subjects for the camera. In their strong, but always graceful forms, ships sum up for us the romantic story of man's eternal struggle with the sea.

Look at the picture of the old-fashioned sailing ship on page 316 and compare it with the battleship on page 298 or with the modern yacht seen on page 301. There is a certain dignity and grace that is common to all of them; it is the beauty that belongs to things that through centuries of experience have become completely fitted for their purpose.

The camera being adept at catching movement, is particularly fitted for dealing with the sea, and it is this ability too that is even more necessary in photographing from the air. To take a photograph from an aeroplane travelling at enormous speed you need a camera with fast lenses, besides filters and other devices to pierce the mistiness that obscures views at great distances.

This is a branch of photography that is definitely new and that has progressed with the amazing advances in man's mastery of the air. For the first time we have been shown the beauties that exist above the clouds where one can look down upon swirling white masses that occasionally part to reveal glimpses of the earth far away below. It is an enchanted land that the camera has revealed to us from the aeroplane.

Photography from the air, however, has other uses than this. For military purposes it is invaluable and in modern warfare it has come to play a vital part. It can also assist the town planner by showing him as nothing else could the net result of his work, while for the archaeologist it can reveal the outlines of buildings that have long since disappeared, by discolorations in the earth that are invisible except from the air.

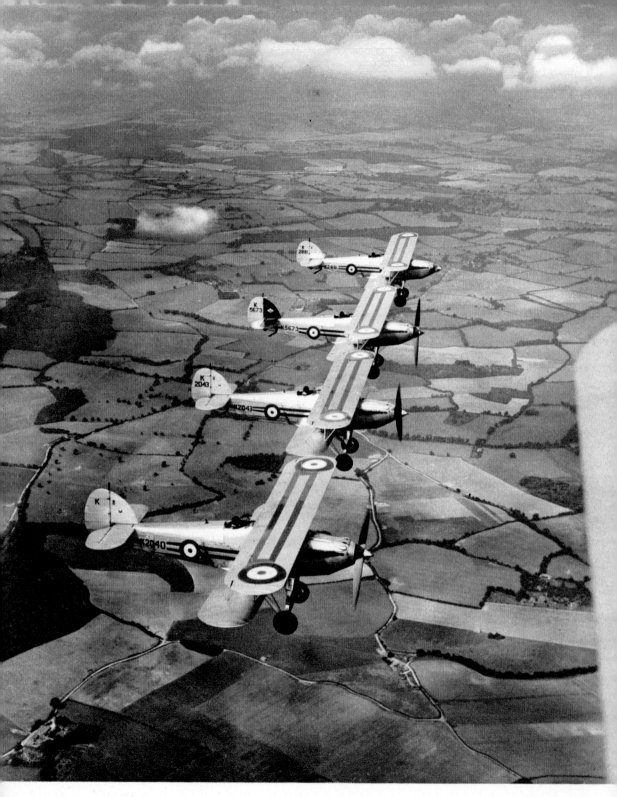

MODERN FURIES   by **CHARLES E. BROWN**

CLOSE HAULED   by A. TANNER

WINGS IN HAWAII   by **M. ARTHUR ROBINSON**

WASHING DAY   by JOHN GABRIEL

SAILS AGAINST THE CLOUDS   by **QUINTO ALBICOCCO**

SMOKE PATTERNS IN THE SKY

by **NOEL GRIGGS**

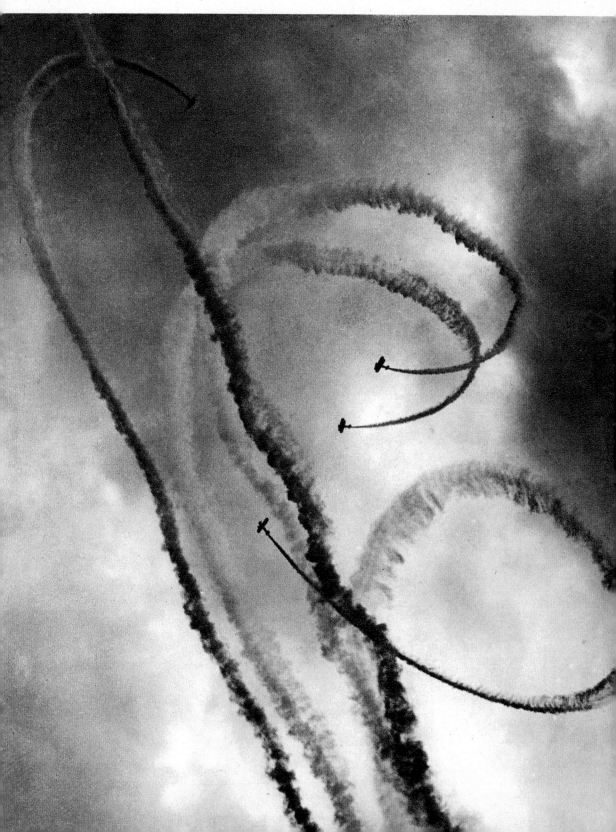

WHITE SAILS

by **TIBOR CSÖRGEÖ**
A "Kodak Snapshot"

Single-rigged vessels, their sails caught by the wind and lit
by bright sunlight, throw curious shadows on the oily water,
while the quayside behind completes the symphony in white.

BOATS AT ANCHOR   by **ALBERT BARRACLOUGH**

OUTPOST OF EUROPE   by **PIERRE-ADAM**

THE CAMERA AFLOAT AND IN THE SKY

The foreground figures emphasize the massive structure of the rock archway and of the pillars at the entrance to the cave. Notice also the contrasts in pale light and deep shadow.

CAVE IN THE SOUTH SEAS   by **M. ARTHUR ROBINSON**

A SPECK ON THE OCEAN   by HUMBERT ANTOINE

THE ROAD TO THE SEA

A striking aerial photograph of the stream of traffic to be found during any fine weekend on the roads to the sea.

by S. BEADELL

SUBURBAN STREETS

by C. E. MURRELL
(Courtesy of Aero Pictorial Ltd.)

SKYSCRAPERS ON MANHATTAN

PHOTOGRAPHER UNKNOWN
(Fairchild Aerial Surveys Inc.)

IN A ROUGH SEA

by F. J. MORTIMER

SEEN THROUGH A NET   by G. MOUNIER

SAILS IN THE SUNLIGHT   by G. M. GREENWELL
                                                (Courtesy of " Daily Mirror ")

FOAMING BREAKERS   by G. V. HERBERT

WINGS OVER THE SEA   by F. CREACAL

A SHIP SETS SAIL   by M. ARTHUR ROBINSON

THE CAMERA AFLOAT AND IN THE SKY

An effective study in grey and white as the gulls, beautifully poised, hover and swoop down over a shoal of fish in mid-ocean.

A SEA BANQUET   **F. J. MORTIMER**

THE QUAYSIDE

by G. MOUNIER

INCOMING TIDE   by R. DOUGLAS PAUL

BARGES ON THE THAMES   by STANLEY

LINERS IN NEW YORK DOCKS

THE CAMERA AFLOAT AND IN THE SKY

The wash of these three flying boats, about to take off in formation, breaks the surface of the sea with ribbon-like patterns,
illustrative of the terrific power and speed of the machines.
Aerial photography is here shown in a most effective light.

FLYING BOATS TAKE OFF

by F. CREACAL

THE TAJ MAHAL   by H. G. PONTING

THE CAMERA AS EXPLORER

*In this section are scenes from many lands in the old
world and the new. Buildings and ruins, snowy wastes
of the antarctic, islands of the south seas, peasant and
other types, all these pictures combine to give us some
idea of the infinite variety of the world we live in.*

FOR centuries men have been satisfying their desire to roam far and
wide from their native land in search of new discoveries, for centuries
they have been bringing home wondrous tales of what they have seen.
Of late years the camera has come to their assistance, enabling explorers
to substantiate the truth of what they state. It has in fact become one
of the most essential items in the explorer's equipment, enabling him to
record his discoveries by a method of guaranteed accuracy and to bring
back a permanent witness of his work.

One of the first expeditions to make use of the camera extensively was
that lead by Captain Scott to the South Pole in 1911. The photographer
on this occasion was Herbert G. Ponting, whose work, although it was done
so many years ago, has never in its own field been surpassed. Some of
his superb studies of the Antarctic are included in the following pages
(see pages 332 and 336) and also in a previous section "The Camera
Goes Hunting" where some of his extraordinary pictures of penguins taken
on the same expedition will be found.

The camera has, in this sphere of exploration, done a great service to
those many of us who have no opportunity for travel. It has enabled
us actually to see what the peoples of far-off lands, of whom previously
we had only heard, look like. Typical figures from several lands are
included in the pages of this section. The picturesque strangeness, each
in their different ways, of the Breton girl on page 330, the Tunisian
shepherd on page 331, or, to those people who live in Europe, of the
old Indian woman showing her bangles, appearing on page 325, is
something that before the advent of the camera we could never have
enjoyed. The camera in fact is fulfilling a double purpose; it gives actual
proof of the existence of far-off things, thus turning exploration into an
exact science, and it gives to the ordinary man and woman a far wider
knowledge of the peoples and places of lands other than their own.

JUNGLE LABOURER   by H. G. PONTING

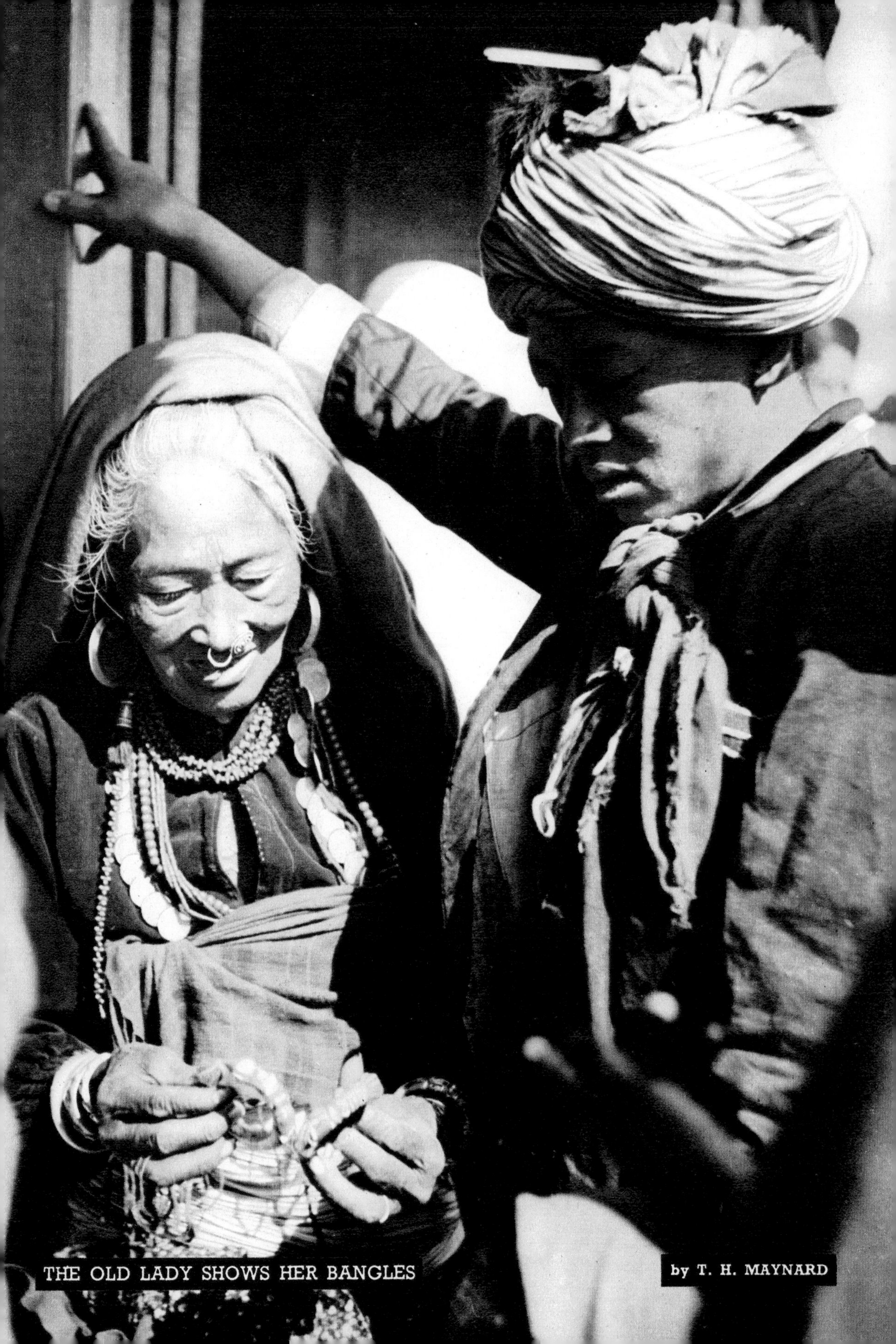

THE OLD LADY SHOWS HER BANGLES   by T. H. MAYNARD

GATEWAY, HALL OF CLASSICS, PEKIN   by ROBERT BYRON

TROPIC PALMS   by C. E. HUTSON

THE GREAT WALL OF CHINA

by H. G. PONTING

THE CAMERA AS EXPLORER

The pose of this girl brings out to the full the picturesque nature of the national costume and headdress of Breton women.

BRETON PEASANT GIRL

by **MARCEL GAUTHEROT**

NATIVE OF TUNISIA   by A. COSTA

BRETON PILGRIMS

by **PIERRE-ADAM**

A fine example of unconscious posing and of how the facial
expressions of a moment can be perpetuated by the camera.

AFRICAN TOILET   by H. W. SWAN

ANTARCTIC GROTTO

by H. G. PONTING

A BALCONY, AGRA FORT

by M. C. PATEL
"A Kodak Snapshot"

CHINESE PRIEST

by R. W. PAULDEN

AMERICAN NEGRO   by BASIL SHACKLETON

KURDISH TRIBESMAN

by **STANLEY JEPSON**

GRAPES FOR TOKAY   by **JENÖ AJTAY-HEIM**

This Hungarian peasant girl in festival costume critically examines
the grapes that will eventually make famous Tokay wine.

ANTARCTIC MIDNIGHT

by H. G. PONTING

THE CAMERA AS EXPLORER

These magnificent ruins at San Juan Teotihuacan, Mexico, give us to-day some idea of the grandeur of the Aztec civilisation that perished at the hands of the Spanish Conquistadores, 1513.

AZTEC TEMPLE   **by A. COSTA**

HAWAIIAN TRAIL

by M. ARTHUR ROBINSON

This picture, taken at the foot of the mountains on Maui, shows an unfamiliar aspect of the romantic islands of Hawaii. The string of pack mules admirably balances the curving line of the mountain crests, while the trunks and leaves of the palms are effectively silhouetted against the background and the more distant sky.

A charming study of a group of young Hungarian girls, clad in their national costume, on their way to the morning service.

OFF TO CHURCH

by **TIBOR CSÖRGEÖ**

STRIDING PYLONS

by NOEL GRIGGS
Studio Briggs
Courtesy of Ferranti Limited

THE CAMERA IN COMMERCE
AND INDUSTRY

*In this section the camera reveals its commercial possi-
bilities. Here are seen advertising photographs of all
sorts from studies of power stations to fashion pictures.*

IF it is true that the camera has revolutionised the art of advertising,
it is also true that advertising has revolutionised the art of the camera.
The association of camera and commerce has been mutually profit-
able, for while modern advertising could never have developed without
the help of photography, photography would never have reached its
present stage of technical excellence except for the very exacting demands
made upon it by advertising.

A commercial photograph, since it is designed for reproduction must
be of the very finest technical quality. Any small blemishes that would
pass unnoticed in individual work, are inexcusable and the commercial
photographer must be prepared to produce work that is flawless. In
learning how to do so he has developed the technical resources of photography beyond the wildest dreams of the earlier experimenters.

But if the commercial photographer has put technical excellence
before everything else, he has not forgotten photographic art. Indeed,
the new medium in which he works has proved particularly happy and
once again the camera discovers for us unsuspected beauty. Fashion
photography, studies of power houses, advertising "stills" are no longer
static representations of inanimate objects; they are glowing, vital pictures
that compare in loveliness with any taken to-day. Consider, for example,
the dramatic vigour of the factory chimneys on page 348. Yet few of
us expect to find beauty in industrial surroundings. Consider also the
dynamic story-telling implicit in the picture of the man drinking beer on
page 357. Yet again this is a subject that is as humdrum as any can be.

It is perhaps in its fashion studies, however, that commercial photography most excels. The modern approach to such subjects is entirely
artistic not representational. The consequence is that here are first
pictures of distinctive loveliness and only secondly, advertising photographs. The examples on pages 351 and 358 are alone evidence of this.

THE CAMERA IN COMMERCE AND INDUSTRY

CHIMNEY STACK SILHOUETTE

by NOEL GRIGGS
Studio Briggs

CIGARETTE FOR MADAM

by BARON
Courtesy of Godfrey Phillips Limited

ANGLE ON THE CHIMNEY

by **NOEL GRIGGS**
Studio Briggs

ANGLE ON FASHION

by **GORDON CROCKER**

Studio Sun
Courtesy of "Ann"

WHITE WAISTCOAT

Studio Sun
Courtesy of Thos. Waide & Son

FUR WRAP

by LEE
Courtesy of Swears & Wells—Studio Sun

THE CAMERA IN COMMERCE AND INDUSTRY

TUNING-IN

by J. H. WILLINK

Courtesy of Philip's Radio—Studio Sun

BRUSHING HER TEETH   by HUBERT DAVEY

POACHED EGGS

by GABOR DENES
Courtesy of Express Dairy Co., Ltd.

BITTER AND BERT

by **HUBERT DAVEY**
Courtesy of The Avenue Press

ELEGANCE

by PETER CLARK

"WHAT'S IT WORTH?"

by **NOEL GRIGGS**
Studio Briggs

AFTER THE BATH   by HUBERT DAVEY

THE CAMERA IN COMMERCE AND INDUSTRY

Here the camera conveys the stress and strain of modern business life with the incessant ringing of the telephone bell.

"I CAN'T HEAR"

by GORDON CROCKER
Courtesy of Raw Products, Ltd.—Studio Sun

SHADOWS OF STEEL
by G. G. GRANGER

BOBBINS

by NOEL GRIGGS
Studio Briggs
Courtesy of Adams Bros. and Shardlow

by PETER CLARK

FASHION FIGURE   by **DOROTHY WILDING**

THE BIRD CAGE

by D. OCTAVIUS HILL

This exquisite study by one of the greatest of all photographers, taken about 1843, is a triumph over technical limitations.

THE CAMERA TELLS ITS OWN STORY

*In this final section one hundred years of photography
are explored. Here are collected some of the photographs that record the development of the camera. They
include some of the very earliest photographs ever taken.
An interesting feature is the historic news pictures that
begin with the Crimean War and end with the Coronation of King George VI. As before, pictorial greatness
has been preferred to mere historic significance or story.*

THE year 1839 marked the birth of photography and in the year
1939 exhibitions were held all over the world to celebrate the cen-
tenary of this new medium of recording which, from its beginnings
as a primitively scientific form of entertainment has to-day become one
of the great industries of the world. This evolution of photography in
a short hundred years is sufficiently remarkable in itself: but it reflects
moreover, the astonishing influence which it has had upon the world,
an influence indeed comparable with that exercised by the invention of
wireless.

In the short and final section of this book which follows, an attempt
has been made to collect some of the outstanding photographs which
have been taken since the birth of this new art—for an art it has now
become as well as an industry. Almost entirely, this attempt has been
directed by a desire to present photographs that are in every way worthy
of contemplation in themselves, photographs which in their day certainly
ranked as great masterpieces. The technical limitations of the early
apparatus are frankly impossible to understand to-day, so easy and so
automatic has become the modern business of taking, developing and
printing a picture. It might be supposed, therefore, that these limitations would have crippled the art of the earliest photographers and made
a comparison between their work and the work of their modern successors
quite odious.

Actually this supposition, reasonable as it may be, is quite wrong. A
glance through the next few pages should prove it. Despite all the
difficulties against which the early experimenters contended, despite the
complete novelty of the medium in which they were working, a

considerable number managed to produce photographs that, pictorially, can rank with any in this book. Take for example the photograph by D. Octavius Hill on page 366. It dates from the year 1843 and its technical limitations are obvious. Yet in feeling and in composition, in the handling and grouping of his subjects, Hill has shown himself to be a photographic artist of the first rank.

It was inevitable that until the comparatively recent development of fast lenses and films, photography should be limited more or less to formal portraiture. Certainly it was in this branch that it most excelled, but some astonishing work was done in other directions. Perhaps the most remarkable, as certainly the most fascinating achievements which it reached in other directions, were the news pictures that record for us scenes from earlier days. In this section a number of these early news photographs are to be found and amongst the earliest are those of the Crimean and American Civil Wars, photographs associated with the names of Roger Fenton and Matthew B. Brady respectively.

A fitting sense of the dramatic is to be seen in all these early photographs and although technical limitations forbade these early workers from attempting the same subjects as those so successfully recorded during the last Great War, the same vital appeal is evident in all. Indeed a very interesting comparison is offered between, for example, the photographs of an 1865 battery on page 374 and of a 1916 howitzer battery on page 381.

These historic news pictures have been carried, in this section, up to the Coronation of King George VI in Westminster Abbey (page 384). This was the first occasion on which the coronation of a sovereign had ever been photographed. Before that date the world had had to rely on artists' impressions of the scene and good as some of these impressions have been they cannot compare, in their intimate reality, with the work of a photographer.

The camera has indeed brought us a new sense. By its aid we can now see into the past. All previous history before 1839 has relied upon hearsay, the written word, and the fleeting impressions of contemporary artists. That state of affairs is past. To-day we can study the intimate everyday life of the late Victorian age in the same detail as we can study the contemporary world. Yet that age is as much part of history as the age of Shah Jehan. And in the future our remote descendants will be able to recall us in all our comings and goings with the same ease as we ourselves now recall our last year's holiday.

THE CHESS PLAYERS

This early collotype by Fox Talb
1839, and may possibly be the
contemporary experimente
showed in all his work a fine s

by JULIA MARGARET CAMERON

Mrs. Cameron was one of the first people to make a commercial venture of photography. This fine portrait dates from 1865.

PORTRAIT OF AN OLD LADY   by **D. OCTAVIUS HILL**

Another fine example of Octavius Hill's portraiture. This
particular photograph dates probably from the year 1842 or 1843.

COUNT CAVOUR   **PHOTOGRAPHER UNKNOWN**

The Peace Congress that was held in Vienna in 1856 was one of
the first historic assemblies at which a photographer was
present. The above study of the famous Italian statesman
Count Cavour, is remarkable both for its unusual technical
excellence and for the sensitive handling of its subject matter.

SIEGE OF SEBASTOPOL   by **ROGER FENTON**

FLORENCE NIGHTINGALE

Roger Fenton was possibly the first of all war photographers, and his pictures of the Crimean War, 1855, one of which is seen above, are notable for their sense of the dramatic. The fine study (seen right) of Florence Nightingale, by an unknown photographer, probably dates from 1855.

TWO STUDIES OF THE AMERICAN CIVIL WAR

Matthew Brady did for the American Civil War what Roger Fenton had done for the Crimean. Although technical limitations did not permit him to take action studies, his posed groups have a vigour soldom seen in photographs of his day.

by **MATTHEW P. BRADY**

HOSPITAL SUPPLIES, 1866

PHOTOGRAPHER UNKNOWN

This photograph shows a hospital supply depot at Potsdam during the Austro-Prussian War of 1866. Every person in this group was required to stand still for a matter of several minutes.

Taken in 1894 during the first war between China and Japan.

FIELD BATTERY IN ACTION

PHOTOGRAPHER UNKNOWN

PORTRAIT OF A GIRL   by H. P. ROBINSON

This photograph, dating from about 1871, is remarkable for its
effective use of lighting—an unusual innovation at this period.

QUEEN VICTORIA

PHOTOGRAPHER UNKNOWN
From the Rischgitz Collection

This early portrait of Queen Victoria, was taken about 1875.

WHITEHALL, 1900

THE MANSION HOUSE, 1902

PHOTOGRAPHER UNKNOWN

These two fine views of famous streets in London provide a
fascinating contrast to the scenes that may be witnessed to-day.

PHOTOGRAPHER UNKNOWN

FUNERAL OF KING EDWARD VII   **PHOTOGRAPHER UNKNOWN**

An historic photograph showing Kaiser Wilhelm II on a white
horse, riding close beside King George V in the funeral
procession in London of King Edward VII on May 6, 1910.

THE MAN WHO BEGAN
THE GREAT WAR

by PHILLIPP RUBEL

This unique photograph shows the arrest of Princip, the
Serbian student, immediately after he had assassinated the
Archduke Franz Ferdinand of Austria and his wife at Sarajevo
on June 26, 1914. This event precipitated the Great War.

A famous picture showing Hindenburg, the Kaiser and
Ludendorf at General Headquarters during the Great War.

WAR LORDS CONFER

THE GUNS SPEAK

PHOTOGRAPHER UNKNOWN
From the Imperial War Museum Collection

A magnificent photograph of a British 8-inch Howitzer battery in action during the long-drawn-out Battle of the Somme, 1916.

This photograph, one of the most dramatic yielded by the Great War, was taken from a British vessel. It shows German sailors scrambling on the sides of the German battle cruiser Blücher, as she was turning over and sinking. She was knocked to pieces by gunfire during the Battle of the Dogger Bank, 1915.

SINKING OF THE BLÜCHER

PHOTOGRAPHER UNKNOWN

DEATH TO THE ASSASSIN!

PHOTOGRAPHER UNKNOWN

The dramatic moment immediately after the assassination of King Alexander of Yugoslavia and M. Barthou at Marseilles, France in October, 1934. An officer has just cut down the assassin.

The Germans entered Austria in March, 1938, preceded by Austrian Nazis. Here is the head of the column at Innsbruck.

by A. COSTA

WOE TO THE CONQUERED!

HITLER ADDRESSES THE REICHSTAG

by BORIS STAHN

Members of the Reichstag listen on March 18, 1938, at the Skala, Berlin, to Hitler's account of the occupation of Austria. He is seen standing below Field-Marshal Göring in the President's Chair.

THE CORONATION OF KING GEORGE VI   by R. SPELLER